THE WAY OF ST JAMES:
GR 65

St James at Moissac

THE WAY OF SAINT JAMES
THE GR 65

Hal Bishop
with drawings and photographs by the author

CICERONE PRESS
MILNTHORPE, CUMBRIA

ISBN 1 85284 029 3

*With especial thanks to Brigitte Pfender, without whose
help this guide would not have been possible.*

*Dedicated to the Confraternity of St James who have done
much to encourage walkers of all faiths and those of none.*

Front Cover:
The chapel of St Michel atop the Rocher d'Aiguilhe at Le Puy.

Back Cover:
Estaing

CONTENTS

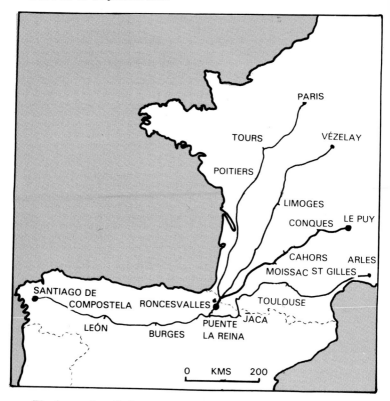

The four major pilgrim routes across France. The GR 65 follows the way from Le Puy to Roncesvalles

INTRODUCTION

The *Chemin de St Jacques*, Spanish *Camino de Santiago*, is but one of many long distance walking routes that that admirable French body the *Comité National des Sentiers de Grande Randonnée* of the *Fédération Française de la Randonnée Pédestre* – mercifully FFRP-CNSGR for short – has designated in the last twenty years. But unlike most of the other walking routes it has been there all the time; having existed for centuries as one of the four great chemins that crossed France from east to west on the way to christendom's third shrine: *St-Jacques de Compostelle* or *Santiago de Compostela*. Third in magnitude of importance, ranking behind Jerusalem and Rome but without doubt top in popular imagination and in volume of devotion.

Of those four great routes the most northerly two, those of Paris via Tours and Vézelay have nearly disappeared, not to history but subsumed into the modern road network. It would be possible to walk them, but rather than the air and the grassy tracks of the *paysage*, the stench of diesel and petrol would be omnipresent to say nothing about the dangerous idiosyncracies of French driving. The most southerly route, that from Arles, is a little better, and the FFRP-CNSGR have recreated a part of it, the GR 653, which runs from just west of Toulouse via Auch and then south-west to Maubourguet. But in truth it is, now, a poor relation; about 150km of lowland walking roughly parallel to the main Route Nationale 124 from Toulouse to Auch which itself chiefly runs over the historic road. Maubourguet itself is still nearly 100km short of the beautiful Pyrenean passage of this route over the Somport pass, which then descends to Jaca in Aragon.

So the GR 65, now part of the E 3 stretching from the Czech border to the Atlantic is the walkers' route; the near 800km from Le Puy to Roncesvalles is, of course, not entirely free of the impingement of a modern communications and transport network. The French in their drive for *Le Modernisme* in the remoter rural parts have misguidedly forced through engineering schemes, and surfaced tracks that rarely see more than the odd tractor a day. Some parts of the way have been spoiled and recently, yet in comparison with the other routes it is a marvellous month's walking.

The Way of St James stretching out westwards on the plateau above Le Puy

It has been said that everyone has two countries: their own and France. True though that may be, which France? Auvergne and Gascony are not the same France familiar to us, their cross-channel neighbours, as Normandy, the Pas-de-Calais or metropolitan Paris. Life is altogether different, more bucolic and thus slower, pleasures are savoured, long and drawn out. If there is reserve it is certainly not the Norman dourness, neither is there the thrust and frenetic haste of the capital. Gravitas and passion are there in equal measure – as may be observed over the 24 hours of any *jour de fête*, or memorial on the anniversary of liberation day – local not national. All this links modern life with past history, weaving in and out of the fabric of those central and south-western regions. Anyone who walks and remains untouched by it is not only very self-contained but must be utterly self-possessed. Yet in no sense is the area of the GR 65 a unity; the Basques in the Pyrenees are quite different from the cattle herders of the Auvergne or shepherds of the Causses. The subtle change as one region blends into another is part of the delight, and no people are more regional than the French. Edwin Mullins, whose *Pilgrimage to Santiago* is one of the better books on the route and its art (though it only really comes alive when he abandons his car and walks a little) commented on Santiago itself, that its impact no more depends upon a committed Christian response, than the impact of the Parthenon presupposes a belief in the Olympian gods. And that is true of the way itself, there is a fellowship of the road. This has been reflected in the astonishing rise of the non-confessional modern confraternities of St James. That in Britain flourishes, having been in existence only since 1983. Anyone contemplating walking any part of any route should certainly consider contacting them for advice and membership – the annually updated guides are a bonus; the address can be found in Appendix III.

HISTORY

That the city of Santiago/St-Jacques de Compostelle is in fact founded purely upon myth, devious mendacity and chauvinism, and that its prosperity is contrary to the Christian ethic it is supposed to espouse and symbolize is an interesting field of study in cultural anthropology. Yet suffice it to say the devotion of the pilgrims making the journey, and the necessity for the pilgrimage to be undertaken was for centuries unimpaired by such ecclesiastical abuse.

Legend

James the Greater was the first of the disciples to be martyred, and the first Christian martyr after Stephen. It is said that he evangelized in Spain but without much success until the Virgin Mary appeared to him at Zaragoza, following which he erected the first ever church dedicated to her, then returned to Jerusalem where he was beheaded on the orders of Herod Agrippa in 44.

The body and the head of the apostle were conveyed by his companions to Jaffa on the coast of Palestine from whence ship was taken, which within a week (!) had fetched up at Padron (Roman *Iria Flavia*) in Galicia on the NW coast of Spain. The companions were jailed by the Roman civil administration until, like St Paul, they were released by an angel. The Roman authorities notwithstanding, a local queen, Lupa, wishing to be rid of them decreed that James' burial should take place at a snake-infested place. However at the sign of the cross the venomous reptiles were extirpated and Queen Lupa converted. A fit and proper burial then went ahead.

Alas, the only evidence for James having been in Spain comes from a corrupt Latin translation of a Greek text. The greatest of the western Christian fathers, St Isidore of Seville, writing in his *Chronica Majora* in the early seventh century does not say that James was ever in Spain. However, the myth was energetically promoted throughout the eighth century, particularly by St Beatus of Liebana in his commentaries on the Apocalypse in 776. The need for a

Abbot Durandus c.1100. Builder of Moissac and encourager of pilgrims

10

saint-protector for poor, backward but Christian Spain was a concomitant of the poverty and bankruptcy into which organized society had fallen – a psychological necessity when threatened by a superior and vastly more accomplished culture. Thus the legend of St James as *Matamoros*, or Moorslayer, was born.

St James having lain undisturbed and undiscovered for centuries miraculously reappears in the ninth century, though the tale comes only from an eleventh century source. A hermit had a vision of a tomb revealed by a star shining on a field, this was related to the local bishop and sure enough a stone tomb was found and duly declared to be that of St James. Alfonso II of the Asturias (791-842) was sufficiently impressed not only to erect a church as a shrine but to declare him the protector of Spain. Around the church the town of *Campus Stellae*, field of the star, grew up. The story emanates from a forged letter of Pope Leo III, the eleventh century source. Similarly the etymology is also false, being almost certainly a corruption of Latin *componere* – to bury; archaeological excavations within the church have revealed the presence of a Roman necropolis.

Legend has passed into established fact and the myth became sanctified, pilgrimages began. With the disappearance of the Ummayad caliphate of Al-Andalus in 961 Northern Spain was left in relative peace whilst the petty-successor states warred amongst themselves. 'Compostela was lifted to the front rank of medieval shrines by a combination of shrewd promotion and excellent communications' (J. Sumption) and, one may add, by historical good fortune. Many immigrants and pilgrims flowed over the Pyrenees along the *Chemins de St-Jacques*. Hospices were plentiful, stretching back along the road deep into France. The great archbishop of Santiago, Diego Gelmirez, the 'catapult of God', who completed the Romanesque cathedral, made it his chief concern, after enriching his archdiocese, to keep open the Frenchmen's road, *camino francés*. South-west France was particularly atuned to the spiritual impulses of the times and witnessed great movements of people. An Almoravid embassy to northern Spain in 1121 was astonished by the number of 'Franks' on the road.

Twelfth century promotion reached its apogee in the so-called *Codex Calixtinus*, otherwise and more correctly known as the *Liber Sancti Jacobi*, because the papal preface of 1124 was as apocryphal as much else to do with St James. The fifth book of the codex is one of the world's earliest guide books. Pilgrims bound for Santiago were told of the four great routes with hints and advice on the peoples and places they would come across. The guide was written by Aimery

11

Picaud, a monk at Parthenay-le-Vieux, near Poitiers on the Tours road. In an age of credulity, when totally specious relics 'recently discovered' could command widespread acceptance and reverence, a phenomenon of the twelfth century pilgrim roads was the establishment of churches and reliquary-shrines near or astride the great network funnelling towards Santiago. Parthenay was just such a place, as were St Leonard at Limoges, St Gilles at Arles and Ste Foy at Conques. All shrewd, if fraudulent promoters of and purveyors to the extraordinary pilgrim fervour of the times.

Fraudulent though the relics might be, the churches were art of the first rank – the sight and sound of the church beautiful were handmaidens of the church triumphant, as the walker will see everywhere on his route. 'Monument to the creative strength of crude blind faith' well describes the roads to Santiago. But medieval man would have found resonance with St Anselm's *credo ut intellegiam* – I believe in order to understand.

The Le Puy route
If we credit Aimery Picaud with codifying, if not creating, the four major routes, it is from Le Puy that we can credit the first recorded pilgrimage. It was that of the Bishop himself, Gottschalk, who went in 951, though we do not know exactly what itinerary he followed – presumably a mixture of old Roman roads and those linking the newer settlements of post-'Barbarian' Europe. Despite the prominence of the Le Puy route, or *via Podiensis*, because of it being one of the four major routes, it is still impossible to speak of the route as being fixed throughout all its history. The political geography of the domains and fiefdoms traversed and the historical mutability of feudal ties led to many shifts between the eleventh and the twelfth century highpoints of the pilgrimage and its desuetude in the seventeenth. Just as the ribs of early medieval vaulting were supported and enhanced by the later addition of liernes and tiercerons, so the four principal routes had many interconnecting links and secondary shrines. Indeed the most visited shrine in Europe in 1218 was neither Rome nor Santiago but Rocamadour in the Auvergne, west of Aurillac. The thirteenth century land-bagging of south-west France's independent Occitan states, that went under the euphemistic title of a crusade, and the later dynastic wars between the Anglo-Gascon Plantagenets and the northern French Capetians and Valois which lasted until 1453, witnessed the building of many new settlements and altered the road pattern from some of the earlier *étapes*. For example the ubiquitous *Sauveterres*, as well as *Castelnau*

and *Salvetat* are generally of ecclesiastical origin or places founded by the military orders in the twelfth century. *Chateauneuf* and *Castet* are baronial foundations often appended with the surname of their founders. Most numerous of all are the *bastides*, new towns of the middle ages and a product of the Anglo-French wars. They generally date from 1220-1350 though some fall outside this period. There are over 300 in Gascony/Guyenne alone.

Between Le Puy and the river Lot the terrain is all above 600m/2000'; always poor, it was rarely in historical contention and today the GR 65 runs more or less exactly along the historical route, sometimes utilising Roman roads such as the Agrippan way, though where parts of it are now the D 987 it has been avoided. The descent to Conques from the heights above it on the north side of the river Ouche would be recognisable to the medieval traveller. Unfortunately having climbed out of Conques the GR 65 goes by minor roads to the ugly industrial centre of Decazeville, instead of further north via Flagnac where a ferry would have been taken, because it is the most convenient bridging point back over the Lot; the route continues to Figeac slightly further north and actually on the river Célé.

There were at least three routes west from Figeac:

1. Via the valley of Célé by way of Espagnac-Sainte-Eulalie, Marcilhac, Sauliac, Saint-Géry and so to Cahors.

2. North to Rocamadour then south again via Gourdon, Salviac, Montcabrier, Villeneuve-sur-Lot and La Romieu east of Condom; this route is more or less followed by parts of the GR 6 and the GR 652.

3. The southern route. This one went by Beduer, recrossing the Lot at Cajarc to cross the dry limestone plateau of the Causse de Limogne utilising Roman roads into Cahors. After leaving Cahors by the Pont Valentré the route ran initially to Trespoux-Rassiels via what is today's D 27, then south to L'hospitalet, Castelnau-Montratier on the D 16 and 19 and thus into Moissac. After the foundation of Lauzerte in 1177 an alternative and increasingly popular route from Cahors went via Montcuq to Lauzerte and then into Moissac, this is what the GR 65 follows today.

The confluence of the Tarn and the Garonne was crossed by ferry to a point just north of St-Nicholas-de-la-Grave, then the way ran west to Auvillar and Saint-Antoine. The GR 65 goes south, crossing the Tarn by the canal viaduct to Castelsarrasin before turning west to cross the Garonne and meeting the historic route at Saint-Antoine.

The way then went via Flamarens and Miradoux to Castet-Arrouy and then into Lectoure. Much of this part of the way has been turned into minor roads but the GR 65 is almost always nearby and parallel when not on the historic route itself. Between Lectoure and Condom the route from Rocamadour, the GR 652, joins the GR 65 south of Le Romieu. West of Condom the way went south of Larresingle crossing the still extant Pont d'Artigues as does the GR 65 to reach Eauze via Lagraulet-du-Gers. After the foundation of Montréal in 1289 the route veered north into it, as does this.

Between Eauze and Aire-sur-L'Adour the N 124 replaces much of the route which instead wends its way through the typical Gascon mixture of vineyards, maize and tobacco fields. Between the rivers L'Adour and Gave de Pau any definitive way is difficult to pin down. It was, and is, a countryside of small villages often dominated by ecclesiastical overlords who were in competition with the secular rulers for the pilgrim trade. South of the Gave de Pau the county of Béarn had a number of routes crossing it. That from Arles passed through its territory, before crossing the Pyrenees into the kingdom of Aragon, its nominal suzerain. The GR 65 goes south and west via Pimbo, Arthez de Béarn, Sauvelade and Navarrenx where it crosses the Gave d'Oloron and enters the Basque country. Just south of Saint-Palais the three northern French routes converged, and a monument allegedly at the right place – though not without its critics – marks the spot. It is just a short distance to St-Jean-Pied-de-Port, the walker will enter the walled town via the Porte de St Jacques and leave it from the Porte d'Espagne to ascend to the frontier just short of Roncesvalles.

TOPOGRAPHY AND ECONOMY

Auvergne

Part of the *Massif Central*, "the water tower of France"; a high plateau separated from the Pyrenees by the Acquitaine basin. The fantastic domed landscape of the *puys* is the product of volcanic intrusions forced up through the underlying rocks. The rocks of the main faults, such as the Allier, which form the impressive gorges, are sedimentary. West from the Velay, the region round Le Puy, is the Devès – another volcanic massif, basaltic; which has weathered to provide pasture almost to the point of monotony. West again, the Margeride is much more wooded, more granite, but it is deeply riven by the gorges of the rivers L'Allier and Truyère. Most westerly of the massifs is the Aubrac which is higher and bleaker than the others; it is almost treeless except where small brooks run in the granite beds where beeches are found.

These upland regions used to grow rye and buckwheat (*segula* – poor soils where only rye, Fr. *seigle*, can grow) on the poor silicaceous soils. They are now almost entirely given over to grazing from mid-May onwards for four to five months. The snow has largely gone by April in the Aubrac, the most extreme region, though temperature variations may still be as great as 20°C in a few hours. With the advent of spring this immense rolling down is blanketed with wild flowers running riot in blazes of colour over the unploughed pastures. July and August can be very hot but it is often superb above 1000m.

Transhumance still takes place; cattle usually cross the Lot at the beginning of the fourth week of May on their way up to the pastures. They are mostly the typical fawn-coloured and dark-pointed beasts of the Rouergue, the area south of the river, and are all garlanded, the leader carrying a huge bell. An annual Fête de Transhumance is held in the town of Aubrac, where they are all collected at the weekend after the river crossing – seen from the gîte at the *Tour des Anglais* it is quite superb. But one of the chief points of interest of the fair is that it is here that the Aubrac herders 'hire' the cows for the summer. They are milked for the famous Auvergnat cheeses whose sale pays for the hire, the wages and hopefully makes profits for the winter months. The numerous isolated *burons* are places of shelter and cheese-making. The custom goes back to the days of the *Domerie*, an order of military monks who protected the pilgrims in this wild area.

West from the Aubrac spurs of land run down to the Lot, created by the fingers of streams flowing south west into the river some 1000m below the plateau.

Quercy and the Lot Valley

Curiously the Lot is not, here, the geographical frontier it ought to be (but see below). Not until east of Figeac is the nature of the *Causse* country really apparent. Between Espalion and Capdenac the Lot gorges dominate the landscape, having worn a bed through the older softer hills, while the many tributary streams create similar deep high-sided valleys. Conques is splendidly situated half-way up a hill between the gorges of the Dourdon and l'Ouche. Trees march with the streams alongside either bank. Decazeville lies in a basin of carboniferous beds which have given rise to an iron and steel industry and the gross ugliness of huge open-cast mines – it really is a black country of coal. The hills are dark, sharp and slaty.

The Lot also demarcates Quercy which stretches from the Massif Central to the plains of Aquitaine. *Haut Quercy* comprises Cahors and the north side of the Lot, *Bas Quercy* lies south of the river. A fault line east of Figeac runs south to Villefranche-de-Rouergue separating the secondary rocks of the Causses de Quercy from the underlying crystalline and primary sediments of the Massif Central. The slaty hills thrust south as far as Villefranche, east it is the red sandstone of the Rouergue. Only at Espalion, itself built of red sandstone, like Estaing, does the Lot touch upon the frontier with the Causses; south and east it is all hard, dry Jurassic limestone. These waterless plateaux 'a broad belt of desert highland' are far and away the most Mediterranean type of terrain the walker will encounter. Winter comes later to them than either to the Auvergne massifs or to the higher Cévennes to the south. Snow soon goes and it becomes very hot. Rainfall does not form itself into streams but sinks into the porous rocks through *avens*, swallow-holes, (see glossary) creating underground caverns – a potholer's paradise. Sheep rearing is the chief activity on the *causses*, migration taking place during the summer months from the Mediterranean marshes. They drink from man-made dew ponds *lavogues* and are folded in enclosures for the night.

The Cajarc Causse lies between Figeac and Limogne-en-Quercy, its trees mainly stunted oaks and maples, sheep graze on the sparse grass of the 'pastures', sub-divided by low drystone walls. Meat is the principal 'crop' of these 'spectacled', i.e. black eye-ringed sheep, wool is very much secondary. The low-lying neck of land between the Célé and the Lot, and the many meanders of the latter are richly cultivated. Farther west the Limogne Causse runs towards Cahors; this has a very different appearance: the plateau is much drier and is dotted with megalithic tombs and markers among the white truffle oaks – truffles are a major enterprise – juniper and lavender. The curious and mostly tumbledown circular stone cells are shepherds' *garriottes* or *cazelles*.

South of Cahors the GR 65 traverses *Bas Quercy* to Moissac, via the *pays de serres*, a series of chalky plateaux crossed by escarpments of harder rock forming spurs of long narrow ridges, the *serres*. The crests at around 200m support sheep, oakwoods and some crops in the clayey soils. South of Lauzerte the area is more popularly known as Quercy blanc where cypresses dominate on the plateaux tops. The

Clustered houses and narrow ruelles in Le Puy

'La Grand Draille' outside Aubrac

A typical Gascon coteau

low-lying rivers form fertile corridors through the *serres*, rich meadows bordered by poplars; slightly higher up the soil supports crops of vines (especially the *chasselas de Moissac*), plums and other fruits, and tobacco. Tobacco for smoking comes from the alluvial soils while that made into snuff comes from the *causses*.

Acquitaine to the Pyrenees
Moissac lies at the eastern edge of the plain of Acquitaine and at the junction of the *Agenais*, the alluvial plain of the Garonne, with the outlying ridges of the Quercy. The alluvial river valleys and their underlying sedimentary rocks date from the tertiary era and stretch south to the Gave de Pau. Between this river and the Pyrenean foothills at Saint-Jean-Pied-de-Port are cretaceous deposits of the secondary era. While the Pyrenees themselves are a complex formation of crystalline and metamorphic rocks of the primary era: gneiss, schists and mica inter alia.

The *coteaux* of the Gascon plain are split by rivers draining into the Garonne. The climate is again very much more temperate, more maritime and thus much wetter than that of the Mediterranean-influenced *causses* only a few miles east – a sharp salient formed by the angle between Cahors, Albi and Toulouse roughly divides the zones. The GR 65 travels right across the fruit-growing département of Gers, which is the centre of the Gascon brandy industry, Armagnac. South and west of Aire-sur-L'Adour maize which first arrived in the sixteenth century predominates, and so rapid is its growth that a second crop of winter wheat is often sown. A hybrid American maize is now the most popular, being used in the cellulose industries that are a consequence of the industrialisation of the Gave de Pau based upon natural gas, as well as for animal fodder. It is an odd sight to see the easy conjunction in which maize and bracken grow. Both Béarn and the Basque country are wet, because of their proximity to the Atlantic and the high mountains. Sheep-rearing and small, mixed farms are still important. The small sturdy *pollocks*, or Basque shetland-like ponies are bred, not for beach rides and the delight of small children, but sadly for the butchers. The slopes of the Pyrenees are naturally clad with indigenous deciduous trees as well as the ubiquitous conifer plantations.

USING THE GUIDE

Waymarking
The route is described from Le Puy to the Spanish monastery at Roncesvalles (*Fr.* Roncevaux), i.e. in the direction of the pilgrimage. Waymarking in France is by means of red and white horizontal flashes; red and yellow or yellow flashes alone mark routes other than the *Grandes Randonnées* (GRs) and should be ignored unless directed by the guide otherwise. Warning signs of crossed red and white flashes are sometimes seen, these indicate that one has inadvertently left the route and indications for change of direction should be sought: these are horizontal red and white flashes with a shorter set beneath with a direction arrow indicating the direction to follow. Waymarking varies from département to département; best of all are Lot and Pyrénées-Atlantiques but the others are generally adequate. At certain places within the body of the guide the sign ◊ appears; whilst most flashes are painted onto trees, rocks or buildings, this indicates a finger-post set up specially. Often at GR junctions they may contain additional information e.g. ◊ GR 65/E 3. Again, they are found with greater frequency in some départements than in others.

Maps
Ideally one should be able to follow the GR 65 from its waymarks and by using this guide alone, but this would be very limiting. Maps are

essential, as much as for the pleasure of orientation and making one's own diversions as for a necessary aid in finding one's position when lost. This guide is based upon the French equivalent of our Ordnance Survey, the *Institut Géographique National* (IGN) 1:100,000 *serie verte*. There are two reasons for this: firstly the route of the GR 65 and all the adjacent GRs are marked on the maps, and secondly all but a few kilometres are covered by only five sheets, whereas more than 25 would be needed if the 1:50,000 maps were used. The essential five are:

50 (5)	St-Etienne/Le Puy
58	Rodez – Mende
57 (4)	Cahors/Montauban
63 (3)	Tarbes/Auch
69	Pau – Bayonne

Figures in brackets after the map number are edition numbers; these are the newer sheets and are distinguished by a lighter green with the legend *Francais – English – Deutsch* above *serie verte*. A new edition of 69 (6) Pau/Bayonne came out in the summer of 1988 and 58 (6) Rodez/Mende sometime in 1989. IGN 69 covering the final, Pyrenean, section also indicates the route descending into Navarra as far as Pamplona; some 40km from Roncesvalles. It is a good day's walk and indicative of the Spanish part of the route (see Appendix II).

The missing kilometres, about 31, can be found on three other sheets. In the order of walking they are:

64	Toulouse/Albi	12km between Castelferrus and Fignan
56 (5)	Marmande/Agen	10km between Saint-Antoine and the D 49 north of Flamarens
62 (4)	Bayonne/Mont-de-marsan	9km between Les Capots and Bacqué

For planning purposes, all but a few kilometres east of Cahors can be found on just two sheets of the IGN *serie rouge* 1:250 000, about ¼ins to the mile.

111 (10)	Auvergne
113 (10)	Pyrénées occidentales

Both the IGN red and green series are widely available in Britain at around £3 and £3.50 respectively, whereas the 1:50,000 blue series is only available from a few specialist map shops. In France the red and green series maps are available everywhere at around FF18 and FF20 respectively. (1988 prices).

Textual Description

Each section begins with the distance walked from the last section and then the altitude. This is followed by, where applicable, the facilities available and a detailed description, if necessary, of the *Gîte d'étape* and where the key may be obtained.

A short history follows the list of facilities; for Conques, Cahors and Moissac I have included rather extended descriptions and a diagrammatic key to their tympana (the semi-circular decorated panel above the door lintel but contained within its arch). They encapsulate not only the atmosphere of the way of St James at its highpoint but remain its *raison d'être* – artistic achievement remains even when the religious fervour that led to its creation has been swept away.

Within the text all place names that can be found on the green series map appear in bold thus: **Aumont-Aubrac**, spelt as on the map – local spelling may well be different. Places that do not appear on the map but are part of the wayfinding description, or will be seen on road signs etc. are given in *italics*, as are the *départements*, rivers, geographical regions, French or dialect words – whose meaning will be found in the glossary.

Directions for turning right or left are immediately followed by N, SE etc where this aids in the route-finding, for it may not always be obvious how far left or right one turns. It is important that the significance of bold square brackets [. . .] is understood. Within them I have either countermanded the route shown on the IGN green series maps because it is wrong, or if correct because it holds little or no merit for the walker. When it is the latter I have indicated in detail a better, shorter or alternative route. Around Aire-sur-L'Adour I have suggested two alternatives to a particularly odd section of the way.

Very little of the walking is strenuous, though there are a few good climbs. I have not sought to set times between the sections as each person has his or her own pace. However the distances between the sections described and the altitudes are given, allowing self-estimation; 4km per hour is often given as an average figure, but in truth a comfortable stride on much of the route is around 6km per hour, still less than 4mph and easily sustainable by a fit walker.

Accommodation

This is rarely a problem. Hotels, all of which provide food, are found even in places where there are no shops. Cheaper and more interesting than those in Britain, it is the room that is paid for, considerably easing the budget of a couple walking. Often one is expected to eat at the hotel – rare indeed it would be to find a poor meal in the unpretentious south-west. Do not expect supper after 8.30-9pm; the French just put up the shutters. Breakfast is not obligatory, is expensive and should be avoided. *Croissants* or various *pains* and a cup of coffee can be had more cheaply from the baker's and at a café. Many hotels have a day off, *jour de repos*, but they will not turf you out if you stay on from the previous day. Similarly shops and bakeries while open on Sundays are often closed on Mondays. The long lunch break from noon until 2.30 or even 3pm is almost universal. All shops and hotels close, usually in August, but sometimes earlier in the summer for their holidays, *congé annuel*.

Gîtes D'Etape

An excellent French institution, perhaps a cross between a youth hostel and a bothy, and often even much superior. They may be old schools, former inns, converted barns, even medieval towers or one floor of an hotel. They all provide cheap lodging for a night. Around FF30 (1988) secures a bed, hot water is available as are cooking facilities. Some are truly luxurious and a few somewhat spartan. They totally obviate the need for a tent, only a sleeping bag is necessary, though blankets and pillows are almost always supplied. Detailed descriptions of how to find the gîtes are given in the text where necessary, otherwise anyone within a small village will know where they are. Some are administered by the local *Mairie* from where the key is obtained; this may seem a problem at weekends and holidays – not so, go to the café nearest to the *Mairie* and ask from whom or where the key can be got. Some *fonctionnaire* or relative will always know; key holders are *Gérant(e)s*.

Gîtes and *Gérants* from east to west:

Montbonnet	*M. Benoit*
Saint-Privat-d'Allier	*Hotel de la Vieille Auberge*
Saugues	*Camping municipal*
Le Sauvage	*M. et Mme Chausse*
Saint-Alban-sur-Limagnole	*Hotel du Centre*
Aumont-Aubrac	*M. Bossuge*
Prinsuéjols	*M. Hermet*
Nasbinals	*Mairie*
Aubrac	*Mme Valery*
Saint-Chély-d'Aubrac	*M. Magne*
Espalion	*Camping municipal*

Estaing	*Café du Chateau*
Golinhac	*Camping minicipal*
Conques	*Mme Bousquet*
Noaillac	*M. Roualdes*
Livinhac-le-haut	*Mairie*
Béduer, *La Vaysse*	*M. Bacalou*
Cajarc	*Mairie*
Limogne	*Camping municipal*
Montcuq	*M. Duflos*
Lauzerte	*Mairie*
Moissac	*Camping Ile du Tarn*
Angeville	*M. Trescazes*
Saint-Antoine	*M. Dupuy*
Lectoure	*Syndicat d'Initiative*
Labusquette	*Mme Duprat*
La Romieu	*Mairie*
Condom	*Centre Salvandy*
Montréal, *La-Boubée-*	
Salle pisant	*M. Ladevèze*
Sauboires	*Mlle Soules*
Nogaro	*M. Daste*
Sauvelade	*Mairie* (? ready 1989)
Ostabat	*Maison Ospitalia*

HOW TO GET THERE

Plane and train are the most convenient for the walker. Long distance coaches pass through Bayonne for the western end of the way, and through Lyon for the eastern end. The relevant airports are Lyon, Montpellier, Toulouse and Biarritz served by Air France, British Airways and Dan Air. However, a new but good cut-price air line called *Air Nouvelle* has started flights to Clermont-Ferrand; not only is it cheap and most convenient, it also affords spectacular views of the volcanic cones, *les puys* themselves.

Le Puy, Figeac, Cahors, Moissac and Saint-Jean-Pied-de-Port are all connected by quick trains to Paris and thus to the Channel, though some changes may need to be made, i.e. at Saint-Georges-d'Aurac for Le Puy. Some smaller places are linked into the rail network; these are mentioned along with bus connections in the appropriate section within the text itself.

Being there

No, they do not speak English! The walking is mainly a delight, but two things will irritate the walker: dogs and *barbelé*, barbed wire.

Everywhere one will see notices, printed signs, even ceramic plaques and forged-iron lettering *chien méchant*. When the yelping brute, who has started his barking long before you are even in sight of him, is abreast of you and foaming at the mouth – evoking the UK's sensible anti-rabies, anti-foreign-animals law – the owner usually turns up and calls him off, informing you that he is not *méchant* at all. Fortunately almost all French dogs are cowards, the author walked from the Channel to Spain and was not bitten once, quite. So while their bark is worse than their bite, it is certainly exercised by the sight of a walker with a rucksac. It is not a bad idea to carry a stick, if only for moral support, and the odd stone in one's pocket. Even the act of stooping as if to pick up a stone is often enough to send curs scurrying away. Although the owners do not mind doing it themselves, and indeed do it shockingly frequently, presumably inducing the national canine psychosis, it is not a good idea to hit their dogs while they are present. Where the dogs on the way have proved to be more than usually importunate I have noted it in the text.

Unfortunately *barbelé* is universal in France, perhaps marching hand-in-hand with the notion of *privé*, though there is no law of trespass as such. The stile does not seem to have passed via cultural diffusionism to the south-west yet; at least it is very rare. Take care and watch your rucksac.

A final note, to end on praise – The PTT phone system is excellent, superior to ours. The tiniest places have phone boxes – often cards and coins. The card phones display the number rung and tell you precisely how much you have left; from both you may ring the UK for a minimal amount, say FF1, sufficient time to give the box number, and have your call returned. Instructions are given in English!

Le Puy: Place du Plot, the starting point of the Way of St James

THE ROUTE

Le Puy 625m
Population 26,000. SNCF rail connections from Lyon are direct on a branch line. On the main Paris – Clermont-Ferrand – Montpellier line change at St-Georges-d'Aurac. All facilities. The map-cum-guide from the Tourist Office is most useful and can be used when leaving. The walker may sign a pilgrim book in the cathedral chapter house, while a mass for pilgrims is said daily at 10.30 am from the beginning of July until early September.

The old town is built upon volcanic outcrops; its narrow twisting streets, which are a joy to wander in, are clustered around the cathedral of Notre Dame. This is reached by a street of steep steps, rue des Tables, and is entered from beneath the plain XII/XIIIc nave. The attractive polychromed cloisters are XI/XIIc while the east end is XVIIc. The extraordinary Rocher d'Aiguilhe is surmounted by the chapel of St Michel, primitive but beautiful Romanesque and is reached by climbing 267 steps from the octagonal St Clair. The late Gothic church of St Laurent preserves one of the three tombs of Plantagenet England's redoubtable adversary, Bertrand de Guesclin (his entrails here). It is being excellently restored. The enormous and vulgar Notre Dame de France was fashioned from captured cannons of the Crimean war; contrast that with the British, who used the metal of their captured guns for VCs. Aesthetically there is absolutely

View backwards over Le Puy from the GR 65

nothing to recommend it, as a viewpoint it is superb. One can eat well here, the town is famous for its Vervaine liqueur, (the dome of Payes Vervaine's distillery in the place Cadelade is the modern landmark in the town – hotels are concentrated here), its 'Jesus' sausages and its lace.

Leave from the *place du Plot*, the traditional assembly point SW of the cathedral and W (behind) of the *Hotel de Ville*. This is the site of the particularly colourful Saturday market which forms around the medieval fountain. Walk west along the *rue St Jacques*. By crossing over the *Boulevard St Louis* the old town is left behind and one ascends the *rue des Capucins*. The first waymark is seen on the right when passing beneath the railway bridge. Turn right at the top in front of the high terrace wall, then after a short distance left into the *rue de Compostelle*. Here one is level with the heights of the cathedral, *St Michel d'Aiguilhe* and the *Rocher Corneille*. Having passed through the suburb of *Les Capucins* turn left opposite a factory onto a cart track. Follow this past a column dated 1621 – it is the shaft of the *Croix de Jalasset*. The D 589 is reached and soon after

5km La Roche 872m
◊ GR 3/65. Turn left off the road, then right to follow a path behind

28

the houses (Dogs!) which continues on a level just below the scarp line above the stream. After about 1km where the GR 3 leaves ◊, the path continues between and across old sheepfolds and drystone walls. Make for a copse passing along the north side of the barbed wire. Leave the odiferous public tip on the left and cross the D 906. After continuing W for 750m above drystone walls turn (N) sharp right, then after another 300m W, left to reach a stream; follow this into

5km Augeac 966m

From the village the main path goes south, though there is a northern alternative (below). The road is followed to **Ramourouscle**. The D 621 crossed to continue passing **la Chapelie Saint Roch** (medieval foundations with later additions and rebuilds) into

5km Montbonnet 1108m

Gîte, camping, telephone

Contour round the village perched on its hill by the east to turn left (SW) onto the D 589. Shortly afterwards turn right, finally off the tarmac at the telephone box to follow a cart track uphill ◊ *Gîte d'Etape*, passing the farm of **La Baraque** ◊ GR 40/65. Before reaching the minor road which runs N-S to the west of **La Visseyre** 1279m a large peat bog is passed to the left among pinewoods (this is the remains of the *lac de l'Oeuf*, almost dry following ecological succession). The northern alternative path joins here.

Northern Alternative Path – Variant

From **Augeac** the road is followed to the large village of **Bains** 975m (Hotels, restaurants, shops). In the middle of the village turn left (W) to pass north of the church onto a field road, passing a wood then a quarry, at the end of it turn right to follow a track (a survival of the pre-Roman road utilized to link Lyon and Toulouse) for 200m before turning left SW off it. Continue on another passing south of **Fay**. Continue into the pine forest turning left (S) then right to join the main path after 500m. Multiple ◊ GR 40/65/65 var.

(Where the paths rejoin, one is in the middle of a series of volcanic cones, a SE-NW fault line where lava has welled to the surface). On reaching the road, turn left (S) for a short distance before heading off SW through trees then open ground in a superb descent, crossing the D 589, to **Le Chier**. Vistas stretch across the Gorges de L'Allier to the plateau of the Monts de la Margeride beyond. Leave the hamlet at its west end by a path which then bears right (N) before descending in hairpins to join the D 589 below the cemetery just outside.

7km Saint-Privat-d'Allier 890m
Hotels, restaurants, shops, camping. Gîte (the large building on the left, the former Ecole Chrétien, just before the road leading into the village). Key from the Hotel de la Vieille Auberge.

Leave the village and the D 589 by going uphill past the PTT then following the path to the left which cuts the bends on the lane leading to *Rochegude 967m.* Pass behind the simple chapel, from where the views down into the gorge are stunning, to descend a slope. Already one can see the pylon concentration which will be passed in front and hear the miserable dogs of the village below. The pine slopes are hot and resinous in the sun; on reaching the D 301 outside **Pratclaux** turn left, the path leads through the village. (Actually there is no real need for this, keeping to the road avoids the dogs heard above. To rejoin the waymarked path turn right between low drystone walls under the first set of pylon lines.) Continue under further pylon lines through fields then steeply down the slope cutting the hairpins of the upper road before following it into

5.5km Monistrol-d'Allier
Hotels, restaurants, shops, camping. SNCF (Paris-Nimes line).

Leave the town by the west, cross the bridge then descend right from the main road to the mill. Cross the river then climb steeply uphill. At the cast-iron cross (olive green!) turn left to pass the rock-hewn *Chapelle de la Madeleine.* Bear right then left through **Escluzels** climbing via hairpins to cross the D 589, continue through pines and deciduous woods passing lush meadows on the right to reach

4km Montaure 1022m
Leave the hamlet by its access road to the south ◊. After 300m turn left off the road onto a cart track which leads south to **Roziers**, then a minor surfaced lane leads westwards to **Vernet**. On leaving this hamlet take the first of the two parallel tracks on the left i.e. the one beside the pines not the one through them, it is not well marked. Passing under two sets of pylon lines **Rognac** is reached (Shelter possible in the *Maison d'Assemblée*). Follow the road NW for 1km then leave it for a path on the left which after crossing yet again the D 589 descends into the town ahead.

8km Saugues 960m
Hotels, restaurants, shops. Gîte at the camping site, on the NW side of the town by the artificial lake.

An attractive town with old stone houses. XIVc Tour des Anglais and church of St Medard.

Cast-iron cross near the Chapelle de la Madeleine

Leave the town westwards by the D 589, having crossed the bridge turn left onto a path, after 100m ◊, there is no waymarking until this point. After another 500m a lane is joined and is followed uphill for 1km to **Le Pinet**, behind the last house a path is followed SSW until

7km La Clauze 1095m
The fortified tower curiously perched on a granite block is XIIc. The vernacular architecture is typical of the Gévaudan.

The path follows the newly surfaced road towards **Le Falzet.** Enter the village by the old road. [It is not really necessary to penetrate the village, by staying on the higher new route the village's dogs remain undisturbed.] Leave by the right-hand fork to reach **Le Villeret** on the D 587. Descend through the village to cross the *Vinlange* then turn right to follow the line of the river valley. The cart track changes to a path under a second set of pylon lines, then back to a track again before descending to a large barn between the two sets of lines which are again passed under. Follow the clear track for 1500m to

7km Chazeaux 1152m
After the first house in the hamlet go right, descending to and crossing the road from **Chanaleilles** (*shop, café-restaurant*), to pick up a stony cart-track crossing and crossed by rivulets following the valley bottom, pylons remain on one's right. After about 1km go left up a heathery hill but to the right of the obvious track (way marks are present but are often concealed by the vegetation) towards a beech clump. Soon, within the beechwood the track is again distinct. Contour round pylons and continue through pines for another 1km. At a glade cross the stream by a 'clapper' bridge to come out onto the D 587. After 1km of road walking turn left onto a bright white sandy track leading in 2kms to

5km La Sauvage 1292m
Gîte, farm meals

From the farm a track leads first south then west and north back to the D 587 at spot height *1304m*. [The loop to Le Sauvage is an 'improvement' on the earlier route which followed the road to the departmental boundary. In truth there seems little merit in avoiding 1km of empty road with good, wide verges in order to detour to the farm unless a night in the gîte is intended. 4km are saved by continuing on the road to point 1304.] After a further 1km one leaves *Haute-Loire* to enter *Lozère* near

3 km Chapelle Saint Roch 1280m
A fountain on the Haute-Loire side has cool, sweet water, camping

Aubrac from 'La Grand Draille'

Descending into Conques

would be possible.

The chapel is a 1901 reconstruction some distance west of the XIIc original and served as a pilgrim hospital.

After 250m a path descends from the road (now in *Lozère* the D 987) left, to rejoin and cross it 1500m on. Descend to a stream by a farm track passing ◊ GR 4/65, before crossing it by a 'clapper' bridge, then another ◊ GR 4/65. Continue SW on a good track through pinewoods leaving the *1209m* spot height to the right. A zig-zag down a scarp slope leads down to the D 987, ◊ GR 65/T M, turn left shortly to enter

6km Le Rouget 1017m

Leave by the wide dusty track S taking the right fork at the old cross before a huge new building. In 1500m the D 987 is briefly rejoined before the route veers left (S) on a lane past the sports field. One passes round the east then the south side of the hospital before descending W into

3.5km Saint-Alban-sur-Limagnole 950m

Hotels, restaurants, shops, buses for Mende. Gîte d'Etape at the Hotel du Centre; a truly magnificent gîte which forms the top floor of the hotel; it is open on Sundays when the hotel itself is closed.

An attractive and flourishing little town with at its centre a XI/XIIc Romanesque church. Red sandstone has been used to give a polychromatic effect to the exterior. Inside there is an interesting series of capitals: leaf foliage and figural.

Leave the town westwards by the D 987, turning right after the sports complex at a sign *Promenade à Cheval*; only then does waymarking begin again. Passing a large sculpted cross one descends in 2km to **Grazières-Mages**. Leave the hamlet by the west then turn left (S) to cross a mill-stream then the *Limagnole* to join the D987 again. After a few metres turn left to ascend by a sometimes boggy path, continuing south to reach **Chabanes-Planes** after a further 1500m. Contour west round the settlement following the tarmac road SSE until a second smaller cross is reached. There go straight ahead on a path following the direction of the telephone poles to pick up a farm track 200m further on. At one point this curves through a field and is reminiscent of an English right-of-way and quite unusual in France. Continue S to

7.5km Les Estrets 940m

Pass through the village to reach the main road, N 106. Go west crossing the bridge over the *Truyère*, then turn left ◊ following a path SW to **Bigosse**. There turn right then left to take a farm track leading SW which ascends a steep wooded slope. The track curves until it runs due west whence it joins a farm access road. This is metalled for the 1500m until its junction with the D 7. This is followed for 3km. [The tarmac can be avoided by walking on the other side of the barbed wire and the road bend short-cut by taking the path to the right after an old and isolated dovecot] into

7km Aumont-Aubrac 1050m
Hotels, restaurants, shops, Monday market, Relais d'Etape, M. Bossuge, 9 route du Languedoc.

  The town is probably a Roman foundation, for it lies on the Agrippan Way linking Lyon to Toulouse. The church of St Etienne is but a remnant of a XIIc priory; there are some fine XVI/XVIIc town-houses.

Leave the town by the D 987 to the west, passing beneath the railway, turn left (S) to follow a path alongside the railway line. Turn right before the large sheds to follow a path uphill SW. On coming out onto a minor road follow it to the right (W) for 400m, then turn left onto a path ◊ which runs through woods S for 2km. At a junction of paths take the right hand fork to join a minor road in 500m. Turn right to follow this for 1km into

4.5km La Chaze-de-Peyre 1040m
Bar-restaurant

Leave by NW taking the lane which joins the D 987 at **La Pinède**. At the junction is the *Chapelle de Bastide* with celebratory plaques adorning its walls. Continue along the road W into **Lasbros**, 400m further on turn left onto a track which descends to a stream – cross it to bear right (N) for 300m before turning left again. After 2.5km, having crossed a stream by a granite 'clapper' bridge, a crossroads at spot height *1178m* is reached. This is *Les Quatre Chemins.* (*café*). The D 987 is followed W for 400m before a left turn (SW) leads one along a boggy track through pine copses. (Often the way is ugly, constrained either side by barbed wire, not unlike the Duchy of Cornwall's effort on the Port Isaac to Portquin stretch of England's South West Way.) Cross a stream then a minor road near a mill, 2km after leaving the pines. (**Prinsuéjols** 1205m is 3km S on this road. *Café, Relais d'Etape.*)

  The way continues on a good track in the same SW direction crossing a stream on granite slabs after 1km. Hereabouts streams and peat bogs cut through the underlying basalt. A further 1km and the cross at **Ferluc** is passed and the D 73 (leading S to **Prinsuéjols** 2km) crossed, continue into **Finieyrols** (beautiful barn). From its west side continue across a plateau, *Montagnes d'Aubrac*, of near-treeless

*Rietort d'Aubrac: ancient stone fountain-troughs
and modern plastic buckets*

fields, divided up by crumbling drystone walls, and less picturesque barbed-wire replacements. Pass over a hill scattered with granite blocks to reach a road where the stream of *La Peyrade* is bridged. Turn left to reach in 1 km

15.5km Rieutort-d'Aubrac 1188m

A granite hamlet with two superb fountain-troughs and a communal oven.

Two routes cross the *Aubrac*, the southern one is the more open but not necessarily the more interesting. It is, however, not waymarked. See Appendix I for a route description.

The northern route leaves the village by the more westerly of the two lanes. Continue SW along it, the river *Bes* on the right and the volcanic puech on the left. The ruined building seen on the right after 1km is the old mill of *Bouquincan*, this is a phonetic corruption of Buckingham and the location probably represents the easternmost limit of Anglo-Gascon expansion in the XIVc. The D 900 is reached after 2km. Turn right to cross the bridge and after a short distance right again to follow a path and then a farm track for 1500m into **Montgros** 1234m. *Gîte; this is run privately by Mme Mangoni at the Auberge de la Maison Rosalie. She is a cook of national repute in France; thus though the menu is a few francs above the average, it is well worth it.* A wide, stony track, *a draille*, leads in 3km to

6.5km Nasbinals 1180m

Hotels, shops. Gîte
The XIc Romanesque church is built of the local brown basalt, its aisleless nave roofed by local schist. Massive columns support the crossing tower. Outside, the southern porch is enlivened with three foliate capitals and a fourth of a fight between an archer and a lancer.

Leave by the D 987 westwards, after 500m bear right off the road to pick up a good track. After a further 2km cross a bridge over a stream. The path continues by a good and obvious drove road which gently climbs, twisting south then west through pastures. After a third isolated barn (*buron*) is reached around the 1300m level, 2km after the bridge, ◊ GR 65/GR TMA, the wide drove road or *La Grande Draille* turns S leaving *Lozère* and passing into *Aveyron*. Having descended east of *Le Royal Ancient Sanatorium* the D 987 is joined at a statue of a tall thin virgin, and followed south into

9km Aubrac 1307m

Hotels, restaurants, Gîte at the Tour des Anglais, key from either of the hotels.
The church, finished in 1220, is transitional Romanesque-Gothic,

though with some walls over six feet thick it really has the solidity of the former. Inside there is an interesting collection of scrap books on the pilgrimage routes. The Tour des Anglais was put up in 1353 in a vain attempt to defend Aubrac from Anglo-Gascon incursions. Today it is a splendid gîte, combining medieval grandeur with modern facilities. The views are marvellous. The transhumance of cattle is still celebrated during the fourth week of May, though somewhat modernised with all the paraphernalia of a fun-fair.

Leave by the D 987 westwards. After 500m go left onto a path, after a stream it becomes a wide droveway leading SW which changes to a rocky path to descend to

4km Belvèze 1144m

The way continues by rocky but shady woodland paths, always descending to join a minor road leading in 1km to

4km Saint-Chély-d'Aubrac 808m

Hotels, restaurants, shops, camping, buses to Espalion. Gîte at the Ancienne Gendarmerie.

The way passes through the small town to the south, crossing the old bridge (on the XVIc calvary a pilgrim can clearly be seen holding his staff and rosary) and immediately begins the climb. Turn right (SW) behind the cemetery. Shortly afterwards the path meets the road, turn left here to walk downhill before picking up a path then the road again into **Le Recours**. Shortly afterwards turn right, descending into oak woods, the path leading into **Les Cambrassats**. Take a sharp left in the hamlet to contour the hill slope round from E to SW. Waymarking is not good here; stay above but keep a parallel course to the telephone lines. A lane leads south. Turning right after 150m a track through high broom cuts off a corner of the lane leading SW. This is followed for 1200m before taking the second junction right, leading in another 1200m to

7km L'Estrade 820m

Just before entering the village from the north go right onto a grassy path between low stone walls to pass round it by the NW. From here it is all downhill to the *Lot* valley, first along the plateau top then through woods for 3km. After crossing a road the way twists and turns steeply to cross a stream before coming out onto another road. This is followed SW for 200m to the junction with the D 557. Cross the road to pick up a path on the left bank of the river *Boralde* before crossing it by a long-abandoned bridge. The D 557 is then followed 2km into **Martillergues**. Turn left after the last house following a path into fields, at a T-junction turn left then right to reach after 750m **La**

The primitive tympanum of the Eglise de Perse

Rigaldie. Here bear left (S) at the communal bread oven, then right passing the cemetery first N then W of it to enter. [If the town is to be visited or supplies purchased continue west into it from the north side of the cemetery.]

9km Saint-Côme-d'Olt 385m
Hotels, restaurants, shops, camping

A pretty town of medieval and renaissance houses and tiny lanes. The early Romanesque XIc chapel is now disused. The XVIc church of Sts Côme et Damien has an odd twisted spire and an ornate entrance.

Leave by the bridge at the SE tip of the town (crossing the *Lot* means leaving *Aubrac* for the *Rouergue*) and turn right to follow the bankside road for 1500m. Then bear left steeply uphill into thick woods. It is rough-going, almost scrambling. In wet weather follow the GR 6 i.e. the road into **Espalion**. At the top near spot height *482m* there are good views across the *Lot* valley. From here descend to the wonderful **Eglise de Perse**, *Chapel of St Hilarian is red sandstone of XIc. The tympanum of the southern doorway is similar in subject matter to those of the great churches on the pilgrimage route: pentecost above a last judgement on the lintel. There are equally interesting capitals inside, and grotesques outside the apse. The bell-cot is typical of the region.* 1km west lies

Espalion

6km Espalion 342m
Hotels, restaurants, shops, camping. Buses to Rodez. The Gîte is a communal tent at the municipal campsite.

Another attractive town sitting astride the Lot, connected by a XIIIc bridge. The turreted chateau is a renaissance building of 1572. The old XVc parish church of St Jean is now the local museum; the current parish church is ugly.

Leave by the rue Camille-Vielland which runs west along the south bank of the river, north of the parish church. The way is clearly marked by the blue and yellow plaque of the French Society for Compostelan studies. After 1500m the D 556 is joined and followed for 1km before a left turn is made onto a newly surfaced road leading to the extraordinary church of

3km Saint-Pierre-de-Bessuéjouls 335m
A simple XIc church with a magnificent chapel on the first floor of the tower. It is reached by the narrowest of stone stairways. The sculpted capitals are stunning as are the IXc altar carvings of the archangels. All in all a joy worthy of superlatives.

From the church the path joins the D 556e and then climbs steeply NW to come out onto a plateau at almost 500m. On joining a metalled lane follow it left (W) for 1200m before turning right (N) to descend to **Beauregard**. Backroads are followed for 3km into **Verrières**. There the D 100 is joined then left west of the village for a path running N then NW which climbs the hillside before descending to the ancient bridge leading into

8km Estaing 320m

Hotels, restaurants, shops, camping 2km north. Gîte at the former medieval chapel of Saint-Fleuret; key from Mme Bregou at the Café du Chateau, the first building on the north side of the bridge on the left. An attractive and well-appointed gîte.

Even for towns on the Lot, Estaing is outstandingly attractive, its huddled stone houses dominated by its XV/XVIc castle. This is now a convent and should be visited, if only for the views from its high towers. Opposite is the XVc church of St. Fleuret; the stone cross outside its south doorway shows a typical pilgrim of St James on his knees before Christ.

From the southern end of the bridge turn right (W) to follow the southern river bank by the minor road for 3km. Before the hamlet of *La Rouquette* (sign posted but not marked on the map) turn left (W) at sign *Danger* to follow a track (which looked in May 1987 as if it was ready to be surfaced). After 750m cross a bridge and turn first right then left to short-cut the hairpin bends of an ascending road. At the next hairpin in front of a farmhouse take the path left (W) to climb steeply. The waymark on a post is not a change of direction as it appears, others further up confirm the path's route. Continue W, away from the road, to pass an isolated cottage with a small *potager*, onto a good terraced path below vines. 1km later the way veers north to come out at a farmstead at c. 520m. Pass between old buildings and in front of a large new one to cross a brook and climb up to reach a road. Follow this NNW for 3km passing through *Le Mas* (*Dogs!*) and a sign-posted turning for *Castailhac*. After a double bend – the last road sign passed is *vers CD 135* – go left up a sandy track then by woodland paths to reach **Massiphs** after 2km. A further 1500m by paths and minor lanes leads N into

15km Golinhac 650m

Café, restaurant, shops, Gîte at the municipal camp site.

A path from behind the church or camp site leads west across fields to **Le Poteau** at the road junction. Continue west on the D 42 into **Les Albousquies**, from here a path leading WSW reaches a minor road after 1km, follow the clearly waymarked lanes linking the hamlets of **Campagnac**, **Le Soulie** and **Carbonnier** into

9km Espeyrac 369m
Hotel-restaurant, shops

Turn left (SW) to go downhill beside the cemetery before crossing a footbridge and turning W to pick up a lane. By easily followed minor roads and field tracks the D 42 is joined after 7km. This is followed for 2km into **Fontromieu**, here bear right to take a lane through **St Marcel**, 1500m later a path descends steeply by stony paths through woods to enter

23km Conques 280m
Hotels, restaurants, shops, camping, tourist office (Syndicat d'Initiative), buses for Rodez. Gîte at former police station, key from Mme Bousquet, rue Emile Roudie, who is known to everyone.

A medieval town dominated by its abbey church, dedicated to Sainte-Foy, begun in 1050. A major centre of pilgrimage in its own right, it contains the typical ambulatory of a pilgrim-church. Inside the vault soars to a height of 22m/72ft and contains superb capitals, though these are difficult to see without binoculars. The sanctuary is set off from the triple-apsed ambulatory by XIIc wrought-iron screens; these are said to have been forged from the fetters of ransomed prisoners who had invoked the saint's intercession – an attractive fiction.

The wonderful tympanum of the Last Judgement over the west portal, 1135, is one of the glories of European Romanesque sculpture. It is best seen in the evening sunlight when its residual colours are no longer muted and the many day-trippers have long since gone.

The waymarking through the town is by means of an engraved scallop shell of St James on wooden plaques. Leave from in front of the abbey's west entrance descending steeply by the *rue Charlemagne* to cross the river by the XVc bridge (220m). Then climb equally steeply through woods, crossing a road to pass the *Chapelle Sainte-Foy*, an attractive building in a sorry state of repair but with excellent views backwards. Continue climbing to reach the plateau top at 550m. Two fields are crossed and a road joined. 250m later at a junction turn left onto the road leading south. In 1500m this joins the D 606, which is followed for 2km until its junction with the D 580 which leads after another 400m S to

8km Noailhac 520m
Café, hotel, Gîte

If the village has been entered (it is regarded as a variant, the main path continuing along the D 580) leave from its west and shortly take a path that angles up the slopes NW then W to join the road at the *Chapelle Saint-Roch* at 601m. Continue W along the D 580 for

The Last Judgement c.1130-40

1. Christ in Majesty blesses the elect with his right hand while with his left he indicates the fate of the damned.
2. Angels sound the last trumpet, others display the instruments of the passion.
3. Mary and St Peter with ecclesiastics and benefactors.
4. Orders of angels ward off the forces of hell.
5. Ste Foy herself being blessed donates the manacles of the captives whom she has ransomed.
6. The Ressurrection
7. St Michael weighs souls whilst a devil attempts to overturn the balance.
8. Abraham welcomes the blessed to the Celestial Jerusalem.
9. Devils feed the damned into the hell's mouth.
10. Satan and his minions receive the damned, practitioners of the seven deadly sins.

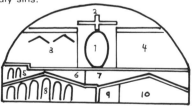

The magnificent Last Judgement at Conques

another 4km; 400m after **Fonteilles** bear left onto a good farm track which contours round the trig point at 595m before descending to cross a road and continue onto **Laubarède**. The views south onto the open cast mines are in the greatest contrast to the bucolic nature of the region around Conques. Cross the road here to pick up (after 100m) the track in fields on the left. The path is very narrow at the field edge and a way may have to be found the other side of the barbed wire. Back on tarmac **La Combe** is passed and shortly afterwards the way continues on cart tracks to **Viviole** where the track to the right, the northernmost of three, is taken to descend from the suburb **Monternal** through modern housing to

12km Decazeville 210m

Hotels (all closed on Sunday, except the most expensive), shops, Syndicat d'Initiative. Buses for Figeac and Viviez 4km hence for SNCF connection to the main Paris-Toulouse line via Brive, or south-east via Rodez and Sévérac.

An ugly XIXc industrial town named after the Duc de Decazes, an entrepreneur who first began the exploitation of the local coal and iron measures. It is dominated by the huge open-cast mine "La Decouverte", over 1km in diameter, which produces a quarter-million tonnes annually.

Do not cross the railway tracks except to enter the town centre. Turn right (W) along *avenue Laromiguière*. After 200m turn right again onto the *Chemin de Nantuech*, the D 963. After a short distance turn left (W) to climb by twisting access roads to houses on the town outskirts. Turn left (NNW) before the D 963 is rejoined, and at a road before **St Roch** turn left then right to go round a new building development. Follow the D 157 (not indicated on map IGN 58) high above the *Lot* valley for 1km. Just before the road veers SW take a path descending N through fields and woods, passing a conveniently abandoned Renault 4 which supports a beehive! The *Lot* is reached ◊ and crossed by either the new bridge or the much more attractive older suspension bridge which is now foot traffic only; ahead lies

4km Livinhac-le-Haut 200m

Shops, restaurants (which sometimes still offer rooms for the night) on the north side of the suspension bridge approach. Camping is 600m up the D 42 towards Boisse-Penchot (the ground is very hard and near impenetrable by tent pegs) the other one at the Club Nautique seems to have closed for good. Gîte, key from the Mairie

Leave from the main *Place* going westwards at the junction of the D 21 and D 627, following the latter for 250m before turning right (N) ◊

onto an ascending path. Minor lanes and paths lead in 2km to **Feydels** on the D 21. This is followed for 400m before turning left, climbing a short distance and turning right (NW). After the farmstead of *Feydel Haut* pass under pylon lines and into *Lot* from *Aveyron* – the waymarking improves considerably ◊ continue W into

6km Montredon 396m

Leave by the road which runs S then W of the cemetery, continue W past a crossroads with a cross on its south side. At the next crossroads turn left (S) under pylon lines and follow the road into the hamlet of *Tournie*. Turn left at the crossroads after leaving the hamlet then right alongside a field track. The way runs west for 300m to arrive south of **La Coste**, paths run S and W to join the D 2 at the Romanesque *Chapelle de Sainte Madeleine, (in the apse there are XIVc murals of Christ in Majesty, flanked by the symbols of the evangelists Matthew and John with Sainte Madeleine and another below.)*

After 100m turn right to pass through **Guirande**, turn right at the last house, then left to take a path running between oaks to a field that was formerly an aerodrome. Turn left (W) to pass behind the former hangar and continue W along the south side of another field, before a path leads N to **Le Terly** on the D 41. Turn left (W) to take a

Sainte Radegonde at St Felix, a crude but telling representation of original sin

path that crosses two streams and becomes a minor road just to the north of

7km Escordier 280m

Follow lanes and paths 800m south to the D 2, turn left (SE) then after 400m sharp right (SW) at the road junction and continue for 1km into **St Félix**, *Church of Sainte Radegonde has a simple but attractive XIc tympanum of original sin.* The waymarked route leaves SW and N from the church. [It is not necessary to follow it, take the D 205 NW for 1200m until it joins the D 2.] From the junction continue by the road for 1750m. The way veers left, off the road at the farm of *Bel-Air*. For the next 4km it twists and turns south of the D 2 though never very far from it, returning to run coincident with it on three occasions. After 300m on the third occasion the N 140 is reached. Cross it and continue 100m W, before turning left up a grassy track for 10m, passing a house with an enormous tree, turning right onto a minor road shortly afterwards. (Though the waymarking is generally good in this section, as it is in all of *Lot*, no change of direction is shown here.) Follow the road N and then W crossing the railway to arrive at the bridge across the *Célé* leading N into

9km Figeac 195m

Hotels, restaurants, shops, camping, Syndicate d'Initiative. SNCF services to Paris and Toulouse, also east via Aurillac. Buses to Cahors, Decazeville, Toulouse.

A delightfully preserved town of 11,000, with many medieval buildings and a number of museums within them. Two churches, the former benedictine abbey of St Saveur and Notre Dame du Puy are Romanesque, altered to southern Gothic. The newly restored collegiate church formerly dedicated to St Thomas of Canterbury, now the église des Carmes, houses the municipal offices in its cloister precincts. An unusual dedication for France, it is one of the few churches founded by Henry II within his empire as expiation for Becket's murder in 1170. The SI produces a town plan that doubles as a guide and historical promenade.

Leave by the south side of the bridge walking west along avenue *Jean-Jaurès*, waymarks lead one via the second street to the left to pass under the railway line and into a farmyard. Climb the hill first W then E to reach a monument commemorating the dead of the war deportees, (145 out of 540). Follow the access road to the road junction, turning left at the sign *Mon. du Cingle 700m*. After another 700m a XIIIc obelisk *L'Aiguille du Cingle* is reached and the D 922 joined. Follow this south for 100m to bear left between large wholesalers' warehouses after the second turning to the right. A tarmac road leads SW for 5km through **Cassagnolle** and **Ferrières** to

9km Faycelles 315m
Bar, buses Figeac to Cahors

Leave by the D 21 westwards ◊. After 2km having passed a turn-off right to Lascamp a track is waymarked to the left. This leads to the *Gîte* at *La Vaysse*. [A confusing wrong direction waymark appears on the D 21. Ignore it.] Continue for 500m to the **Mas de la Croix**, ◊ *Gîte et Camping 400m*, 50m further on take a left fork, ◊ GR 65/651, and continue the 800m into Béduer. (the village may be avoided by a recognised variant: 500m after **Mas de la Croix** turn left by an iron cross up a narrow shady path which joins the main route 500m south of the village of)

4km Béduer 280m
Café, shops, rooms, camping, Gîte at La Vaysse (above) is a communal tent.

Leave by the SW on a lane which parallels the D 19 to the north, after 500m continue straight on by a path. The tarmac which has dominated the way since **Figeac** gives way to fine walking on good paths, often shaded. A short stretch of road is met 600m on, go left then right then left again in a short distance. 2.5km later follow the D 38 left (S) for 250m before turning right. Similarly at **Puy Clavel** turn right at the road to follow it for 100m before turning left off it. A further 1km leads over the D 19 into

9km Gréalou 370m
Hotel, restaurant, shops, Buses Carjac to Figeac.

Leave by the lane west of the church ◊ which leads to the cemetery, passing this on the south, and continue W 1500m to a point where a cross and dolmen are seen. Turn left here (S), continuing downhill to cross the D 82, bearing left. A path passes farm buildings to reach at a crossroads the hamlet of

4km Le Verdier 316m
From the crossroads there are two routes into **Cajarc**: the main route West by the cliff *cirque*; the variant east by woods.

(a) – at the crossroads with the waymark *variante* (4 yellow parallel flashes, 2 horizontal, 2 vertical) go right by a lane NW for 1km to join the D 82, which is followed left (SW) for 150m, crossing the D 17. At farm buildings turn left (S) crossing minor lanes, in 2km join a road for 100m which is abandoned at the lip of the *cirque* to follow the track downhill into Cajarc.

(b) – follow the waymark *variante* S as directed, on a lane until the D 19 is joined. Follow this S for 50m before turning off onto a track S then SW for 2.5km to rejoin the D 19 on the eastern outskirts of

6km Cajarc 160m

Hotels, restaurants, shops, banks, Syndicat d'Initiative, camp site, Gîte, SNCF buses Cahors to Capdenac.

Leave from the west end of town taking the road past the campsite S towards the railway, but do not pass under it; follow it past allotments. After 300m take a path to the right which climbs to the D 19. Follow the road S for 250m, and opposite the ruins of the XIIc *Chapelle de la Madeleine* take the road straight ahead into **Andressac**. After 800m turn right to follow the D 19 W over the suspension bridge then left (S) into

4km Gaillac 180m

South of the Lot, between here and Cahors, the Causse de Limogne is an area of dry limestone, waterless though not featureless. It is the part of the way that is most Mediterranean; after Moissac, south of the Garonne, maritime Atlantic influences are dominant.

After the cemetery the path turns left, to climb E then W, before continuing through a scrub forest of oak, box and juniper S and SW. Often shady and enclosed, the path is shining bare white worn limestone, but well waymarked on drystone walls, trees and the exposed rock. After 3km a larger track W of **Mas de Couderc** is picked up which leads SW for 500m before a turn of 315° is made and a path leading W downhill for 500m before turning S is taken. The stony path leads after 700m to a newly restored house then continues S 1km into

6km Mas del Pech 340m

Cross the D 79 and shortly afterwards turn right, continuing W for 800m. At the third junction turn left (S) to reach **Bories**. Follow the road WSW for almost 1km. At the junction with the lane giving access to the D 19 go left (SE) onto the path – not the field track alongside the woodland edge which is first and seems more obvious. After nearly 1km turn right (SW) to pass **Dalat** and after another 600m join the D 143. Follow this SE for 300m to contour round a farm, almost turning completely round to walk NW through fields (beware sprinklers in dry weather). Continue W to reach the D 911 after 1500m, cross it and continue by minor roads to the D 24. Turn right (N) opposite a large communal pond and attractive *lavoir*. After 50m the way continues W, 500m south of the centre of

The attractive lavoir and pond at Limogne-en-Quercy

8km Limogne-en-Quercy 310m
Hotels, restaurants, shops. Gîte is a communal tent at the campsite.

From the D 24 near the *lavoir* go W to cross the D 19 after 500m. (*Hotel Bellevue* at the SW corner of this crossroads obviates the need to go into the town if only food is desired – *menu du jour* recommended.) Continue W 2km to **Ferrières**, at a junction at a cross take the southern fork. At another junction 250m later take the northern fork, continuing W to pass through scrub woodland before going N through two gates marked *Fermer le Clédo* and then veering round W again.

Cross a minor road after 1km, joining a second minor road after a further 800m to follow it westwards for a short distance before continuing by path for 200m. A right-angle turn left (SSW) leads after 1.5km to a road into **Varaire**. This is followed a short way before turning right. The D 52 is joined 600m later at

7km Laplane 320m
A good track leads westwards from the D 52 at the junction with the cross. After 2.5km it becomes a path bearing right (SW) at the sign *Privée. Defense d'entrer*. 2km on it reaches

4.5km Bach 310m
Café, restaurant, shop

From the village follow the D 19 SW for 600m, turn right off the road

The Lot valley above Livinhac-le-haut

onto a grassy field path which turns right (W) 800m later onto a very good track, this is a Roman road, the *Cami ferrat*. The way westwards is obvious, the *cami* crosses the D 42, D 55 and then the D 26 at

9km Mas de Vers 255m

The way continues, obvious as before but now more north-westerly as it sweeps back up towards the *Lot*. The D 10 is crossed and about 1km later a minor road reached, after an old and tumbledown *lavoir*, and followed left (W) then N to a bridge over a stream. The D 6 runs parallel on the west bank. But do not cross here. Take the road uphill for a short distance before turning left onto a path running alongside the east bank of the stream. Pass two mills then turn left to cross the stream. Turn right (N) onto a lane crossing another stream which leads to the junction with the D 49. This is followed SW for 500m, including the stretch coincident with the D 6. Where the two roads diverge follow the D 6 NW uphill for 800m.

[The 1983 IGN map No 57 (4) Cahors-Montbauban, is slightly wrong here, though the wayfinding is not as difficult as it may seem. One can of course cross the first bridge to join the D 6 on the stream's west side, following past the point of junction with the D 49 to pick up the path. But the true way is uphill on the D 6 once it leaves the D 49, not some path to the north as the map indicates.]

Leave the road before it turns left through a right-angle, veering right onto a narrow path; if it is not visible because of high vegetation three waymarked telephone poles indicate the way. Turn right ENE onto a good track 150m on, follow this for 500m before taking a left fork – the route on the map now equates with the route on the ground.

After 1km cross the road leading to **Flaujac-Poujols** and continue on a stony track NW for 1.5km to join the D 22 west of that village. After only a short distance take the path that runs south of the road westwards to *La Quintarde*, the attractive buildings and lawns of which are passed on the left before the D 6 is joined. Follow it N for a few metres turning right at the junction, then left (N) to follow a stony track between houses to short cut a bend on the D 6 before crossing it obliquely. Continue on dirt tracks following the crest of the spur NW for 4km; the last 1km is surfaced and descends steeply to the Lot, crossing the river by the Pont Louis-Phillipe to enter

17km Cahors 125m

All facilities including Syndicate d'Initiative. Campsite for tents on the east side of the southern end of the pont Louis-Phillipe, even if it does not look like it.

Lauzerte: Gîte in the medieval tower

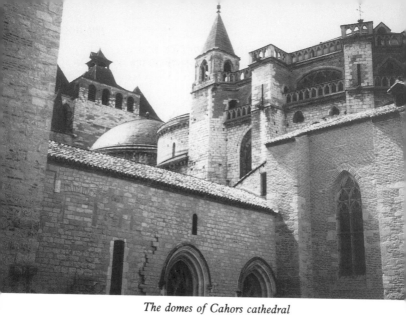

The domes of Cahors cathedral

The capital of the *département*, a bustling town of 21,000, which is famous for its medieval bridge, the *Pont Valentré*. Originally one of three such bridges, it is now rather out on a limb beyond the railway. The old town lies east of the ubiquitous boulevard Gambetta – this is in fact the statesman's home town – attractive though somewhat rundown; its restoration is not yet the equal of Figeac's.

The XIIc cathedral of St Etienne is distinguished by its two massive and typically Perigordian domes, and the absence of any flying buttresses. The interior is uninspiring; yet the tympanum over the north doorway, once part of the main façade, and now dreadfully neglected is of the highest artistry. It was carved about 1135. The cloisters are XVIc, the final fling of Gothic, and among other fine carvings show an argument between two pilgrims. Also of interest are the museums in the Bishop's palace, the church of St Barthélémy and Pope John XXII's tower, over 100ft high. The SI plan of the town is an excellent guide to its history.

Leave by the *Pont Valentré*, turning right once over it to take the first road left, *rue Capelle*, the D 27 which climbs past the *Ecole Agricole*. A path then goes left at the beginning of a hairpin bend. Using the drain as steps, the path then continues to the *Croix de Magne* overlooking the town. From the cross take the road W, then SW at a

The XIIc Cathedral of St Etiènne.
The tympanum over the north doorway.

Ascension of c. 1135

1. Christ in Majesty clasps the book of life.
2. Angels announce miracles to (below) ...
3. ... the apostles beneath cusped arcades
4. Mary points to her son
5. Four cherubim emerge from clouds greeting Christ and supporting his Halo.
6. Events from the life of the cathedral's patron saint, Stephen: arrest, trial and stoning.

crossroads to turn left after 100m before a new bridge. Follow a new road south, flanking but fenced-off from the large new by-pass. Soon a tunnel leads beneath it, the arc of an access road is followed almost full circle to continue S on a road signed No Exit with a waymark below.
[This should be the definitive way, but may change once the bypass and its approach/exit roads are all open in 1988.] At the outbuildings of the farm of *Fontanet* go left onto a path uphill through fields and trees. Right (W) and left (S) turns lead down to

5km La Roziére 220m
After a new house turn left E onto the tarmac road and continue E on a track, then veer left onto a path through bushes before turning sharp right (S), *not* downhill back onto the E-W track, to reach a lane which leads to the D 653. Follow this W for 100m then left along the D 7 for another 100m after the junction. After a little bridge turn right (SW) to follow a good path uphill which leads in 3km to

6km Labastide-Marnhac 300m
Leave by the road running SW from the church, turn left (S) onto a good track before D7/67 diverge. After 500m the way itself splits, a

waymarked *variante* goes off left on good paths into **L'hospitalet**, 4km distance. (*Shop, restaurant, Gîte of rural simplicity at the old school.*)

The main way continues straight on, descending to and crossing a stream, becoming a grassy path and reaching a road running W from **L'hospitalet** after 2km. The *variante* rejoins here, the way continues westwards by a good field track, the old hill road, which keeps to the crest of the spur which runs NE-SW for 6km. After the first 1km of this follow a lane NW for a short distance, then turning through a hairpin S to stay on the crest. Cross a tarmac road 3.5km later to turn first W then N to descend by a path via **Baffalie** and the D 7 to

10km Lascabanes 180m
Shops

From the church ◊ take the lane towards *St-Géry*, instead of crossing the bridge continue W by a path which leads uphill and through woods to come out on the *Lascabanes-St Pantaleon* road. This is followed for 750m to a junction where the left fork is taken SW. Shortly afterwards the *Chapelle St Jean* is passed. (Inside is a pilgrim book which contains notes and news of recent pilgrims/walkers and information on the way itself.)

Continue by the stony path for 1.5km to a converted windmill, now a water tower. Turn right (NW) to cross **Les Gravedis** access road (*dogs!*) reaching the D 37 shortly afterwards. Follow this NW for 400m before turning left for 1200m. At a junction turn left (S) to join the D 4. Follow this for 1.5km then the older track uphill, parallel and just N of it to descend (Sign: *Gîte – Tel 22.90.49*) into

7km Montcuq 180m
Hotels, restaurants, shops, campsite. Gîte at La Gougne. Buses to Cahors and Lauzerte.

An attractive little town of 1200, with a ruined keep perched at the top of its promontory.

Leave by the D 28 southwards but having crossed the small stream continue straight on uphill by a well-shaded path. After 1.5km a lane is reached, take this right to rejoin the D 28 which is followed S for a short distance. When it turns W continue down an access road straight on, signposted *Château de Charry 0.8km*. After 400m turn right onto a path through trees, cross the drive to the château and continue on S to cross the D 28 once again and go on downhill to join the valley road after 300m. Turn right to follow it SW for 300m then continue straight on by a grassy path for 400m. Turn left to cross a stream by a footbridge hidden among brambles. The path climbs SW to a farmstead where the road linking hamlets is followed. Clearly visible ahead on its hilltop, is

7km Montlauzun 220m

Leave by the lane south which descends to the D 45 at a crossroads. Turn left (S) for 200m before turning right to climb steeply between vines and cornfields, and then underwood to reach a plateau top. **NB** Here one leaves *Lot* and enters *Tarn-et-Garonne*, where the waymarking is rather less adequate. Continue SW for 800m to a 3-way road junction, then straight ahead for 350m. Leaving an area of *Prop. Privée* fenced-off on the left, continue by path straight on W through woods. On joining a lane it is followed for 600m, through **Rausson**, downhill. Halfway down into the valley turn right (W) opposite a large corrugated-iron barn. The grassy track is followed round the slope contour passing beside two huge poplars to climb up to a farm. Descend S from the farm to the D 54.

[This is a route change not shown on the map and a disgraceful one. The obvious green road/hollow way leading SW from the farm will lead one astray abetted by the fading waymarks, later on it becomes impassable, totally overgrown. It is regrettably not the only one between here and the Pyrenees.]

Continue by road 2km westwards into

7km Lauzerte 280m

Hotels, restaurants, shops, campsite. Gîte in one of the three medieval towers, key from the Mairie.

Another Quercyois hill-town with its medieval stone houses clustered around the church of St Barthélémy, and the adjoining place de Halle newly restored.

Leave the road SW and turn left ◊ to descend by the cemetery, cross the D 953 to follow the D 81 over three bridges; shortly after the road turns sharp left go right uphill on a green road. (often very wet and overgrown and thus impassable, so go instead up the field edge on the left, then on the orchard edge to the right.) On reaching a road at the hilltop, turn left to follow it 500m past a pottery and a four-poster dovecot; 50m on turn right down a good limestone track. This comes to a 3-way junction; the obvious paths are left uphill through an orchard and right downhill past a new house which is chained-off and signed *Prop. privée*. Do not take these, go straight on by a narrow path into a field, following its righthand edge. An interesting ruin, the *Chapelle Saint-Serin-du-bosc* is left 80m on the left before the way climbs to reach a road which is followed right for a short distance then S 300m. Continue straight on by a path to descend to a farm, where a lane leads S 1km across a stream to the D 57.

Turn right to follow the D 57 for 1300m. After a bridge turn left up a green road (also sometimes overgrown so go up beside it at the field edge) which becomes a lane at a farm building. Follow this lane to a road junction 700m on, there turn left (SE) for 100m before turning right to descend into fields. Turn right then left in the field, not waymarked but easy to see, before crossing a stream. A newly-surfaced lane is followed for a short distance then a line of waymarked telephone poles leading NW. Turn left 300m later to ascend through woods then orchards to join a lane leading S to the D 2 east of

10km Ferret 180m

(**Lacapelette** 1.5km S on the D 2 *shops, hotel-restaurant*.) Take the D 2 for 600m to pass through the hamlet before going left at the first junction, then left again shortly to descend into a valley through vines. Take the road at the bottom left (E) for 20m and then turn right off it just below the little green bridge. Go uphill through woods to pass behind some buildings and take a farm road to the left for 150m. Turn right to pass behind the next group of buildings to descend through vines and trees westwards. At the bottom continue by the dusty track S round a mudbrick building to ascend to a minor road. Turn right (W) and in 400m reach

4km Saint-Martin-de-Durfort 200m

NB From **St Martin** until near **Moissac** the *balisage* is very *individualiste*: it is all upside down!

Leave by the road running SW; 100m after crossing beneath pylon lines turn left to weave through vines descending steeply to the D 16. Cross it then bear left to go steeply uphill under the same pylon line previously crossed, to reach the crest of the ridge. Follow the track eastwards for 1200m to a road junction. Take this right for 200m then go left (SE) at the next junction. Follow this through **Couynou** for 1km along the top of a narrow spur. Turn right by a path, which though difficult to see is waymarked, that descends steeply to a stream in the valley bottom. Having crossed the stream, veer to the right (NW) to pick up a path behind newly-dug clay water-pounds. The upcast from these which are constantly recut has obscured the uphill path. If, as is quite likely, you are unable to find the path or are cut off from it, get through the narrow width of woodland, once over the stream. Beyond lies a clearing with pylon lines running through it. Follow them downhill, at the lowest point on the ground the path will be found. Follow it uphill through the next band of woodland to come out onto a minor road, which is taken left for 150m then right to reach the church of

5km Montescot 185m

Take the path W from the church to pass the cemetery on its north side. Descend SW to cross a stream, the path joins a road running due south. After 2km, at the hamlet of *Delbes* just north of the main D 927, the way goes right [not left as on the map] to cross the road before following it SW for 200m on its tree-lined verges and then turning left.

(**NB** See below for alternative approach)

Having turned off the D 927 turn right (S) at the next junction, 400m later continue S from the crossroads by a path that leads after 1km to the D 101. This is then followed E for 250m before taking a path S before *Sembelle*. After 500m turn left, E again, onto the next road for 250m before turning right (S) to reach the north bank of the *Tarn* in 750m. This is followed W for almost 3km, passing under the railway to reach the canal viaduct, the way goes S from here, but the town must be visited so follow the canal N then W 2km into Moissac.

[This is not a good approach to **Moissac**; once across the D 927 any westward road can be taken into town avoiding unnecessary kms. The only exception is for walkers going to the campsite or the good *gîte* there. In that case follow the official route to the canal viaduct, then cross it before following the road along the south bank of the *Tarn* 1km westwards to reach the campsite/*gîte* on the *Ile du Tarn*.]

14km Moissac 80m

Hotels, restaurants, all facilities. SNCF on the main Bordeaux-Toulouse line.

A lively town but not very attractive; the canal at least providing a very pleasant entrance and exit. However, the exception is the abbey of St Pierre, XVc brick onto the original XI/XIIc work. Its cloisters and astonishing south doorway are breathtaking. This, the third magnificent tympanum of the 'Via Podiensis' of the Camino de Santiago, is framed, unlike those of Conques or Cahors, by a completely sculpted and decorated Romanesque portal. It was moved from the west façade in the XIIIc.

The cloisters (buy the combined ticket for museum as well) were nearly all knocked down to make way for the railway in the XIXc, as happened at St Pancras, Lewes, Sussex. This would have been an incomparable loss, for they are among the most beautiful in Europe. The aracaded columns are alternately single and double and of varying colours. The centre and corners are pillared and are carved with saints in low relief.

Moissac: the distinctive engrailed door jambs of the south portal

The Abbey of Saint Pierre - the south doorway

Vision of the Apocalypse 1125-1130

1. Christ in Majesty holds the book of life with his right hand raised in benediction. He is surrounded by the symbols of the four evangelists:

2. Winged-man of Matthew

3. Lion of Mark

4. Bull of Luke

5. Eagle of John

6. Seraphim

7. The 24 old men of the Apocalypse in three tiers, all turned towards Christ, clutching their musical instruments.

8. Eight rosettes between ropes strung from the mouths of two flanking monsters.

9. A single carved pillar of three intertwined lions.

10. St Paul and Jeremiah

11. St Peter, the abbey's patron saint

12. Isaiah

13. Three orders of foliage in the arch soffits

14. New testament scenes: Annunciation, Visitation, Adoration of Magi, Presentation in the temple, Flight into Egypt and fall of the idols.

15. The Damnation of sinners: devils torture adulterers and a miser. The death of Lazarus at the rich man's feast.

Moissac: Cloister capital, the anunciation to the shepherds

From **Moissac** pilgrims normally crossed the confluence of the rivers *Tarn* and *Garonne* to reach **St Nicolas-de-la-Grave**, continuing north of the present route via **Auvillar** to **St Antoine**. It is possible to follow the old lanes but the proximity of the *Autoroute des Deux Mers* makes this somewhat unattractive. The waymarked route now runs some way south of the historic one before joining it at **St Antoine**.

Leave the town by the canal towpath eastwards. Access to it is easiest, appropriately, by the *Pont St Jacques*. Cross the viaduct 2km on and continue on the western towpath for 4km – there are no waymarks but nor are there any problems. The last lock passed is *Ecluse 19*, then turn right by the bridge, 70m after the cemetery onto the *avenue Léon Brun* (faded waymark) of

6km Castelsarrasin 85m
Hotels, restaurants, all facilities. Campsite and Syndicat d'Initiative. SNCF Bordeaux-Toulouse line. Sadly the town does not live up to its romantic name, only the XIIc church of St Sauveur and a few XVc houses are of any interest.

Cross the town in a SW direction reaching the *Mairie* in the main square. Leave it then by its western edge via the *rue du Gaz* where the waymarking picks up again. Turn right by the very scruffy youth hostel to follow the road for 750m, then turn left onto a lane bordered by poplars crossing a small bridge. Keep left on the steeply embanked side of the *Garonne* through orchards before turning left onto a road which joins the D 12. Go along it W to cross the river by the new bridge south of the old suspension one. Turn left to contour round **St Aignan** (*café, shop*) E then S to reach the D 26 which is followed SE for 800m, turning right off it before the sign of **Castelferrus**. Take the track between houses uphill, through a narrow dale; it is often boggy and overgrown. In 1km, coming out onto a lane go right to a road junction 250m later. Here turn left (S) and after 50m right onto a field track. 400m later at another road junction turn left to follow the road SSW via *Moundous*. Cross a stream and pass beneath pylon lines to reach the hamlet of *Jauberts*. The way goes north to the farmstead of **Doudous** before turning west to take field tracks then short stretches of road into Angeville.

[The fields are often very wet and muddy, when conditions are bad the minor road west of *Jauberts* is the best route.]

11km Angeville 135m
Gîte

Cross the D 63 to leave by a track leading NW reaching a stream after 1km. Cross it and continue to join the road from **Caumont**, near where the pylon lines cross it, 500m on – the wayfinding is tricky. The road is followed S for 600m, then turn right (W) to pass through the farmstead of **Ginestous**, continue SW on good firm farm tracks to reach a minor road after 1.5km. Follow this right (N) for 250m, then left on field paths via a farm, *Boubêne*, to cross the D 15 and into **Gayssanès**. Pass the church and cemetery by the north to take a track running left of an extraordinary dovecot before turning right (NW) at a deserted barn. Ford a stream 400m on, continuing due W, crossing a minor road 750m later. The track continues with poplars on the left and vines on the right, then along field edges with woods on the right, to the north, before joining a green road. At a junction with a minor road go right (NW) for 250m to reach the hamlet of

7.5km Fignan 160m

Continue NW for 1.5km to join the D 93, taking it north for 100m before turning left opposite a farm, *Tapas*. Go uphill for 350m passing vines on the left to reach a track on the ridge top. Follow it SW for 800m. On joining a minor road follow it right over a stream to reach the D 67. Veer left across it ascending W, 600m later join a minor road at a farm leading SW for 200m. Then turn right onto a farm road leading to **Berteillé**, but before the outbuilding bear left to

59

follow the woodland edge for 400m. Then turn right (N) into the dense wood – wayfinding tricky. Turn left after 500m onto a farm track and follow it for 800m to the crossroads at the farm of *Sartre*. Go straight across to reach a second crossroads 400m on, turn right (N) along the lane for 250m. Where it veers left continue ◊ on a dirt track, which leads N along a ridge top then descends and turns W through woods crossing a stream to reach the D 89 after 1.5km. Cross the road ◊ and climb up to

8.5km Bardigues 150m
Café.

Leave the village on its west side by the D 11, following the road SW for 300m before turning right (W) onto a minor lane. After 1.5km this goes straight across another country lane to descend through woods to a crossroads on the D 88, ◊ GR 65/E 3 (!). Continue W on the road passing a pretty mill to join the D 953. Turn left crossing a bridge, and leaving *Tarn-et-Garonne* for *Gers*, poor waymarking for better, continue SW into

4.5km Saint-Antoine 75m
Gîte – nowhere indicated but at the east end of the village; known to everyone for it is at the house of M. Dupuy, le Maire. Meals can be taken en famille or cooked for oneself.

Although rejoining the historic route here, that goes via Flamarens and Miradoux mainly on surfaced roads, the waymarked route goes north through the typical Lomagne countryside of intermixed woods and fields.

Leave the village by a farm track leading NW ◊. After 1200m turn right (N) going steeply uphill to turn left at the next road junction. Continue W past the farm of **Peyrautillon** to a road junction 1.5km on. Here go left (WSW) for 400m before turning right (W) onto a good track ◊ descending through a mixed wood rich in hornbeam, *Bois Grand*. The high-sided muddy banks of a stream are crossed on a none-too-safe wooden footbridge. Continue in the same direction to reach the D 30. Go S along it for a short distance before turning right at a cross to reach *Berné*. Turn left (S) to descend to a water pound ◊. At the bottom turn right for 80m to ford a stream, then take the further left of the two tracks going uphill into the woods. Half-way up the hill turn right in the middle of the wood (it is well waymarked). On emerging from the wood go left along a field edge; keep left passing vines and cherries on the right to enter woods again for a short while. Cross the ridge crest SSE between different crops in fields, entering woods after passing vines on the right. Remain on the top, passing woods and fields on either hand to emerge onto the road at spot height *202m*

8km D 49 202m

Go S 50m to a crossroads to take a path right, then shortly left (SW) leaving a mud-brick building to the left. Descend through woods to cross a stream. Continue in the same direction uphill through a copse. On coming out to vines go right; the path actually contours the field edge but is probably impassable, so make for the top right-hand corner through cornfields to reach a minor road on the ridge top. Cross it and descend alongside a long line of tall poplars; though obvious because of the vegetation the way is not always easy to follow. 600m on turn right and cross fields to an isolated wood which is contoured N then W. A stream is passed and the path leads to a minor road. (A left turn and 2.5km S lies the attractive town of **Miradoux**, *shops*.) Turn right and after 200m leave the road for a farm track left, passing through **Conté** then a building.

[IGN 63 is slightly inaccurate here, the path lies about 250m further N than is indicated.] The way turns right (NW) for 200m on the track that leads to spot height *130m* before turning right (SW), crossing a lane after 400m and reaching the D 19 after another 900m of often boggy ground. Turn left (SE) along the road for 150m, then turn right down the drive leading to

6km Château des Fieux 120m

An amazing XIXc confection, an eclectic building of more charm than grace with its mixture of Gothic, Renaissance and even Tudor.

At the farmhouse in front of the chateau follow the path right which contours S between the park and the farmland before continuing E on a wooded bank. Turn right (S) on a field track which becomes a path then joins the D 23. There turn left (E) and follow it for 200m before turning right ◊ to ascend to the imposing ruin of **Château Gachepouy** (*built 1585, the last blow of the middle ages but with classical innovations*)

[The route between the castle ruins and La Salle as shown in IGN 63 has been superseded.]

Turn right ◊ at the castle to descend by the historic track which joins the D 23 at the bridges over the river *l'Auroue*. Follow it W almost into **Castet-Arrouy**, turning right just before the village sign onto the grassy field track between maize and corn fields (both castles are visible from here). On reaching a belt of trees after 300m bear right to follow the track N past a ruined farmhouse. 700m later turn left to follow the path for 500m along a hedge before joining the

D 245. Go north along the road, but before **La Salle** turn left (W) into woods. After 500m having passed several concealed hides, used for shooting wood-pigeon, bear left onto a farm track which joins the D 218 ◊ which is followed W 1km to a crossroads. Turn left to take the SW road (after 100m a lane leads in 300m to the right (NW) to **La Busquette**, *Gîte*) which becomes a farm road descending past buildings and through tobacco fields before climbing up to the N 21. Cross this road to take the minor lane SW ◊ which after 2.5km of undulations reaches

12km Saint-Avit-Frandit 180m

Bear right at a junction after the church ◊ onto the track leading to the **Château de Lacassaigne**. At the entrance go right onto a path contouring the château on its NW side. Soon it veers left (S). At a mill ford a stream leaving a water pound on the right to go uphill by a stony track to the left. Pass a number of newly restored (formerly abandoned) houses to reach the D 248 after 1.5km. Continue straight across on the most southerly of the three tracks. Veer right onto a path after 700m to cross a stream before ascending onto a ridge at a road junction. Turn right to follow the road for 700m. At the farm of *Jouancoue* turn left to descend by a track, first through a huge orchard then via a hollow way overcast by laurels and cypresses. In the valley bottom at a junction with a house turn right (W) along a lane for 400m then turn left to climb up to the Tour du Bourreau, ◊ *Gîte*, of

7km Lectoure 200m

Hotels, restaurants, all facilities, Syndicat d'Initiative. Buses to Agen, Auch and Toulouse. Gîte at 18 rue St-Gervais; key from SI, south of the cathedral at the Hotel de Ville until 6pm. Outside office hours, or weekends and holidays, from 5 rue St-Gervais. The street runs downhill NW of the cathedral.

The former capital of the Armagnac, Lectoure is a very attractive walled town of narrow streets perched on its promontory, and occupied continuously since the Iron Age. The former cathedral of St-Gervais et St-Portais was begun in the XIIIc and repeatedly altered throughout the centuries; it is now being restored. The former Bishop's palace houses the Mairie, the municipal museum and the SI.

The countryside around is of limestone cut by deep valleys, green and wooded. Fields are mixed, with vineyards, fruit orchards and cereals. The higher plateaux are bare and dry.

The official route, for some unfathomable reason, sweeps south of the town before doubling back along the railway line to cross the river *Gers*.

[Ignore the official route, the historic way is quicker, easier and more attractive. Leave from the west end of the main *rue Nationale*, follow it left, then right into the pedestrian *allé de Montmorency* under the ramparts and below the hospital. It joins a lane that snakes downhill, then traverses a level crossing to join the waymarked route where the D 7 crosses the river *Gers*.]

Turn right after 100m ◊ to follow the river bank a short distance N, then turn left to reach the D 36 400m later. Follow this road N for 400m then turn left (W) ◊ to follow a track leading after 2km to the **Château de Mirail**. Pass two huge plane trees before the château and turn left to take a path through vines, then turn right ◊ in the middle of the vineyard and 100m on turn left ◊ to resume the westerly direction. Pass through the farmstead of **Mirlande** to take a well-shaded stony path to **Verduzan** and continue S to join a minor road.

[IGN 63 is slightly inaccurate here, not showing the route S of **Verduzan** as being on the road until the calvary west of the crossroads.]

Turn right to follow the road 600m W, continue over the crossroads for 100m before veering right ◊ at a calvary. For 1.5km the path goes NW traversing a vast field on a slight rise. At a farm track turn left and after 600m enter

9km Marsolan 170m

XVIc church with a bell tower that is more a castellated than an ecclesiastical structure.

Pass the church on its north side to take the lane steeply downhill into the river valley. Cross the bridge after the crossroads and continue straight on uphill through fields to reach a hedge-belt of trees. Follow this closely on its north side, bearing left with it S to reach a ridge. At the top turn right (W) under power lines, shortly afterwards coming out onto a minor road north of **Cauboue**. Follow this for a short distance, but where it turns north, continue W on a good track above fields for 2km, on what is a good survival of the historic road, to join a road just short of

4km Montravail 175m

Continue westwards on the lane for 600m (50m beyond is **Abrin**, *a restored XIIc chapel of the Knights of St John. Dogs!*) Turn right ◊ onto a farm track (N) to go up-and-down over wold-like country. The track becomes a path between hedges and across fields to enter a wood after 1.5km ◊. Ascend into it, turn left (NW) at the top of the wood ◊ to reach a road after 750m. Turn right onto the road for 100m then left ◊ off it to follow a path through vines and oak plantations, turning right after 700m to follow a track W and N 1.5km to the west side of

5km La Romieu 185m
Hotel-restaurant, shops.

A tiny but lovely township of 550, dominated by its huge collegiate church of the early XIVc, which includes two large towers and a double cloister. Only one other large tower remains from its cardinal-benefactor's palace.

Leave the town by the D 41 700m west. 100m after a calvary take a path bearing right, which continues W for 600m to join a minor road, and follow this N for 200m by turning right. Turn left at a crossroads onto the drive to **Château de Maridac.** Follow the drive to contour the château N and W onto a path bordered by oaks which reaches a minor road in 500m. Follow this S to the D 41, go W on this for 50m before crossing it to descend S to a stream and the climb uphill to

5km Castelnau-sur-L'Avignon 166m
A medieval village reconstructed after its destruction in June 1944 in a German reprisal for resistance activity.

Cross the road at the east end of the modern village to descend to a stream, once across it veer left (S) ascending through trees and hedges and a farmstead (*Dogs*) to reach the ruined XIIIc *Chapelle Sainte Germaine* on a lane. Turn right to follow it W to **Le Bardieu**. [Slight inaccuracies on IGN 63.] Pass to the right of the château then via a tree-lined alley and track to come out at a 3-way road junction. Go left (W) downhill, then rise up over a stream to turn sharp left (SE) after a second group of buildings at **Fromagère** (*Dogs*). Go right uphill (S) at vines to pass in front of a farm on the left, *Borde Neuve*. Follow the access road S to the D 204, turn right to follow it for 500m, then turn left on a track leading to **Barada**. Follow the lane to the D 7, turning left for 50m, then cross it to continue S for 250m. Then turn right onto a path, crossing a stream and coming out by the walls of the Carmelite convent. The official route inexplicably bypasses the town, but from the convent go NW along the *rue de Prouillon* to enter

11km Condom 75m
Hotels, restaurants, shops, all facilities. Campsite, Syndicat d'Initiative. Gîte in the rue Caduet, round the corner from the Centre Salvandy where the key can be obtained from the Concierge in the second courtyard. The centre lies south of the cathedral and is reached

Dovecot typical of those in Quercy blanc

Larresingle, a fortified town in miniature

from place Voltaire going west along the rue Jean Jaurès. Buses to:
Toulouse, Auch, Agen, and Mont-de-Marsan.

The town is typically Gascon, the centre of the Armagnac industry.
Its centre is well preserved, now pedestrianised. The XVIc cathedral of
St-Pierre is one of the last great southern Gothic churches, flamboyant
in all its decorativeness; the cloister and the bishop's palace are all of a
piece, the musée de L'Armagnac is nearby.

The official route from the convent continues SW to the D 654, then
turns left (S) along it. 300m later turn right to pass through *Cité
Bellevue* and cross the main D 930, then the river *Baise* by the
footbridge. Turn right to walk N along the riverbank, the campsite is
on the left. (There is no merit at all in this route.) The way crosses the
main D 931 in front of *St Jacques*.

[To leave from the town, cross the *pont des Carmes* continuing S
and W along the *rue de la Republique*, *place du Cardinal* to pick up
waymarks south of the *avenue de l'Armagnac* near *St Jacques*.]

Follow the lane 200m SW to pass under the railway then along a
minor road 3.5km WSW to a 3-way junction. (For **Larressingle** *a tiny
place but one of the most beautiful villages, the "Carcassonne du
Gers". Completely walled with only one tiny gate the episcopal castle is
XV/XVIc with a church within its keep.* Follow the road 1km NW ◊.
To rejoin the main way return via the D 507/278 ◊.) Go straight

Conques: a knightly pilgrim

*Pont d'Artigues, a romanesque bridge built to carry
the pilgrim traffic*

across at the junction to follow a path downhill through hedges and
vines to arrive, having passed a large house, at the D 278. Continue
straight on at a crossroads ◊ to the historic bridge over the river
l'Osse.

7km Pont d'Artigues 83m

*A five-arched Romanesque bridge; the nearby medieval pilgrim hostel
run by the Order of the Knights of Santiago has completely vanished.*

Cross the bridge, and at the crossroads turn right (N) and follow the
road for 700m, turning left off it before **Pellefigue** to follow a field
track with a hedge on the right. [IGN 63 is slightly inaccurate, the way
runs south of that actually marked between **Pellefigue** and the
crossroads on the D 254 NE of *Lauraët*.] Continue through woods
onto a road which is utilised for 20m as it veers westwards round a
bend. Shortly afterwards, passing a cross then a house on the right,
the path runs alternately between woods and fields to reach a
crossroads after 1250m. Turn right (NW) for 500m, then left (W) at
the next road junction, passing S of the isolated church of **Routges**, to
cross both arms of the D 254 after 1km. Continue westwards by the
lane through **Lasserre** (*notice the unusual bird-scarers in the
cherries*).

Just after the sign to *La Glezia* (a farm whose precursors run back to Gallo-Roman times; many excavated finds are in the museum at *Auch*) leave the surfaced lane to descend by a grassy track, crossing a stream and going uphill, still due west, onto a farm lane at **Pages**. Before the lane goes right to join the D 15 continue on tree-lined grassy tracks veering left to pass the **Château de Lassalle-Baqué** to join the D 113 which leads into

10km Montréal 130m
Hotels, restaurants, shops, Syndicat d'Initiative. Buses to Toulouse and Condom.

One of the first 'bastides' of Gascony, built 1289 on the site of a prehistoric hillfort. There are attractive lanes and houses, and especially the arcaded square with its medieval church, restored in the XVIIc.

Leave the town by its SW corner. Turn left off the D 15, do not cross the river, ◊ descend to the stream and continue S (1km SW of the town is the *auberge de la Mouliotte*, a campsite and *ferme Auberge*). The tarmac gives way to a track which veers left uphill to pass a farm, *La Boubée-Sallepissant* (*Gîte*); 2km south of the town the path turns left and joins a minor road which it follows E with vines on the right, cornfields on the left. Turn right (S) at a road junction 400m ahead, vines now on the right. [IGN 63 is slightly inaccurate indicating a route S then E rather than E then S.] Continue down a drive to

4km Château de Montaut 100m
Contour the château E then S to pass under an old railway bridge. Then go west along an alley overshadowed by huge trees – waymarks of shells hammered into trees – for 500m; turn left (SW) at a pond and go uphill to reach the D 230. Follow this left for 100m then turn right onto a path to pass through vines and then along a belt of trees. A good hard track is joined for 150m before reverting to a path which crosses the D 29 ◊. The path continues W between vines and a house twisting left and right to cross the D 31 onto a lane. [Again IGN 63 is slightly wrong, the way crosses the road at the junction south of that marked.] Continue W for 300m before turning left through vines on a green road leading to **Lamothe** (*XIIIc tower, XVIIc church*). The route passes a waymarked water point (*eau non potable*); however, *eau potable* is indicated at the entrance to the cemetery. Pass N and W of the church taking a track downhill W, but before the river *L'Izaute* go left onto the line of the old railway, (Notice in 1987: *Nouvelle itineraire. Suivre le balisage – Eauze 2H.*) which runs S and W for 2km.

Turn left onto the second road crossed by the railway, and follow it S for 1.5km. Before the crossroads near **Bretagne d'Armagnac** turn right for 100m then left (S) at **Higne** onto a good track, passing yet more vines on the right, and the cemetery at some distance on the left. Just before the D 29 turn right to walk for 100m between vines and trees before turning left to cross the road obliquely to take a tree-lined drive to a large house at *Jaulin*. Turn right (W) before buildings to follow the track SW at the edge of a vineyard. On reaching power lines step down a terrace and turn right (W). Shortly afterwards leaving a water tower on the right go straight over the crossroads at the D 29. Then turn left into the new hamlet of *Cuhercle*. After 1km, with **Eauze** continually visible, turn left (S) to pick up the course of the old railway line, which is followed left for 150m. Turn off this right to reach the campsite *Moulin du Puy* after crossing the river *Gelise*. Traverse the site to climb back up to the course of the railway, leaving the viaduct on the left continue right (S) for 750m; at the factory turn right onto the D 931 and enter

9km Eauze 160m

Hotels, restaurants, shops, all facilities. Campsite at the Moulin du Puy (above). Buses to Pau, Auch and Toulouse.
An attractive town of 4400 souls with a bustling market. The cathedral of St Luperc is Gothic, built partly in brick, of 1500. There are also some fine arcaded half-timbered houses.

Leave by the D 931, turning right after 500m to follow a track SW; it can be very boggy when wet, then walk beside and above it on vine terraces. A short stretch of road follows before the way reverts to track, crossing fields via barbed-wire gates all well waymarked and all in the same SW direction. Cross a stream on a footbridge of railway sleepers after 3.5km; soon a hollow-way leads to a wooded area. Mount clay steps to the left into a field and follow its edge. A ruin is passed after 800m, and the way goes downhill with vines on the left to a newly surfaced road; cross it to enter a wood which is soon left to join a road after 80m. Turn right (NW) to follow the road for 1km before turning left through vines, (CAUTION, unmarked electric fences) to go downhill. Cross a stream and turn left to follow the hedge-line at a field edge uphill to a track. At the top of the track ◊ *Gîte 800m* (**Sauboires**: *Gîte right, limited food available there.*) Continue straight on (S) on an enclosed path and through hedgeless fields to join a farm track leading to a junction on the D 122. [IGN 63 is wrong between the D 122 and the D 109.] Take the roads into

11km Manciet 120m
Hotels, restaurants, shops.
The inn La Bonne Auberge is the former Hospital St Jacques.

[The official route runs W and N of the town and has neither the merit of historical accuracy nor that of practicality as it adds quite unnecessary kilometres. So leave the town by the N 124, and after crossing the river *Douze* continue on the D 522 *Manciet-Nogaro* road to **Perès** where the official route is rejoined. The D 522 is unmarked on IGN 63; it is the straight road S of the N 124.]

Continue by the D 522 SW for 600m and then turn off left taking a farm track downhill, across fields and two streams before going uphill again with a wood on the right. Turn left at a lane then right again to join another lane which runs into the D 522 just before the bridge over the river *Midon* to enter

8km Nogaro 100m
Hotels, restaurants, shops. Gîte north of the sawmill off the N 124. Buses to Pau, Auch.

Founded by the archbishop of Auch in the XIc the church is of that date, though damaged in the XVIc wars of religion.

[Again the official way runs N and W avoiding the town. Ignore it, except if going to the *Gîte*. Take the D 153 W rejoining the way at **Labadie**.]

Turn left off the D 153 onto a track which is followed over the river *Juranne*. 800m on at a road junction, go straight on before turning left (S) to join the N 124 over the river *L'Izante*. Follow the main road for 250m before turning left to follow a good track for 800m, then bear right (W) to emerge after 1km onto the D 152. Cross it, then turn left for 20m before resuming the same direction by turning right again to continue through fields by hedges. Then go through woods NW then SW to reach a minor road after 3km. Follow it SE for 800m until the farmstead of

11km Sansous 150m
Turn right off the road to take paths S and W through fields and trees to pass a farm on its south side after 700m. Turn left (S) onto a track, shortly afterwards ◊ *Gîte*. After 800m is *Micoulas* (*Gîte is the old farm building on the right; go to the farm left. It is primitive and replaces the tent shelter blown down in the hurricane of 7 June 1987.*) Continue straight on for 400m to where a farm, *Brana*, sits on a minor road. Turn right (W) ◊ to follow paths across the D 169 to pick up a track leading downhill to a stream. Turn left to follow alternate riverbanks S for 1.5km to the hamlet of

5km Manet 110m

Turn left to follow the road a short distance E then right ◊ onto a good firm track for 2km. Turn right (WNW) two paces before the level crossing to follow the track parallel to the railway for 2.5km. Turn left to cross the very busy D 935. Continue S down a track for 500m, then veer round with it half-right. Continue SSW for 1.5km to cross a bridge then turn right and follow a track to a farm, there turn left only to turn right again 300m later and approach another farm. Turn left at a junction before it, where there is a curiously shaped oak and follow the lane to join the D 107 at a bridge over the confluence of the *L'Adour* and *Le Lees* (*campsite on the bridge's north side*). Cross the bridge to the 3-way junction of

9.5km D 107/39/22 80m

Turn right to follow the D 39 300m NW to a monument to eight *Maquisards "Massacrés et carbonisés par les Allemands 13 Juin 1944"*. 50m further on the waymarked route turns left uphill.

[The official way around Aire-sur-l'Adour is perhaps one of the less interesting parts of the GR 65, and especially the section between the D 39 and the N 134. Two alternatives follow:

i) into town to pick up the official route at **les Capots**

ii) by country roads S and E of the town to pick up the official route just W of **Latrille**.

Route i) Follow the D 39 from the monument 2km NE, now in *Landes* into

2.5km Aire-surl'Adour 80m

Hotels, restaurants, shops and all facilities, campsite. Buses to Pau, Mont de Marsan.

A pleasant and ancient town of 7200 pop.; an episcopal see from c. 500-1933, though little of interest survives to bear witness to its long history. The cathedral was started in the XIIc but has XVc vaulting and much later post-reformation work; the XIXc decor is particularly ghastly. The brick-built Ste Quitterie du Mas, XIII-XVIc, contains a vast Romanesque crypt and the IVc white marble sarcophagus of the saint. The Gothic doorway again displays a last judgement.

Leave the town by a road leading SW to **Les Capots**, parallel but south of the N 134. Join the main road after 1km, continue for 300m before turning right (W) on the D 2 to pick up the official route.]

Turn left (SE) after 250m to take the minor road through **Le Boué**, continue SW for 1500m to *Lourine*, go left at the junction, continue S then W until the next road junction. Turn left (S), after 700m the lane gives way to a track which is followed S for 1300m, turns right (E) then continues essentially S, crossing the D 62 after 1km and the D 375 SW of **Latrille** 3km further on at the east end of **Bacqué.**

[*Route ii)* Continue NE along the D 39 400m, then turn left to ascend steeply to the plateau at a road junction. Turn left to follow lanes via **Guillon** S for 7km to the D 260 west of **Ségos.** Turn right to cross the N 134 and continue W for 1.5km to a crossroads with the D 62 at the north end of **Latrille.** Cross the D 62 to take a lane for 300m to a junction with a track. By turning left (S) the official route will have been rejoined, 500m further on the D 375 is crossed at the east end of]

13/10km Bacqué 180m

Cross the D 375 and continue S. At a junction 700m on veer left off the road onto a track for 1300m passing a farm and turn right to reach a road 350m later. Turn left to follow this road S for 100m, then right to pick up a track leading first W then S to **Douelle**, and then by a lane continue SW to cross the D 11. (**Miramont-Sensacq** lies 1200m W, *Hotel-restaurant, shops.*) Lanes lead S then W to join the D 314. Turn left and after 50m right to cross the road, continuing by lanes into **Galette.** Then turn right to take a lane NW, after two farms the lane becomes a track descending from the plateau to cross a stream near the church of **Sensacq.** (*formerly dedicated to St Jacques, a beautifully restored XIc church which still has its very rare total-immersion fonts.*)

Take the lane S from the church which joins the D 11 and is followed W 1km into

13.5km Pimbo 195m

The oldest bastide in Landes, established in 1268, the church of St Barthélémy is the only one of three that remains; it has a fine Romanesque doorway and capitals.

Leave from the east end of the village by a lane descending SE near the cross and after 200m turn right on a hairpin to take a track which descends steeply to another lane. Follow this across a stream, out of *Landes* into *Pyrénées-Atlantiques*, the south-westernmost *départment* of France where the waymarking is excellent. 1km later join the D 32 [IGN 69 indicates only the totally pointless *variante*] which is followed 3.5km into

6km Arzacq-Arraziguet 230m

Hotels, restaurants, shops.

Another bastide of XIII/XIVc Anglo-Gascon foundation, though all remains of its gridded plan have gone, except for the main street.

Leave the town by going straight across the main street from the point of entry, down a narrow lane between houses to a junction at trig point *238*. Bear right onto a road which becomes a track as it descends to cross the river *Le Luy de France*, continue into **Louvigny** and **Lou Castet**. From this village follow the road S to join the D 279 into **Fichous-Riumayou**. [The historic road linked **Lou Castet** to **Garos**, this was originally waymarked but has been temporarily abandoned. However, a fading *mauvaise direction* can still be seen on a corner post 900m SW of Lou Castet, near where the route turned NW on a track beyond a farm. This will be restored in time but for the moment follow the road S to the D 279. IGN 69 is wrong between **Lou Castet** and **Uzan**.] Take the main road W from **Fichous-Riumayou** 2km into

10 km Larreule 120m

Romanesque church of St Pierre. All trace has disappeared of a Benedictine abbey which dominated this important staging-post on the way.

Turn left to pass the church and then right to cross the D 262. The way goes W and S to cross the river *Le Luy de Béarn* before turning NW to reach **Uzan** after 2.5km. Follow lanes W 2km into **Géus d'Arzacq** and then further W – there are two ways both clearly marked – a further 1km into

8km Pomps 130m

Church of St Jacques with an attractive statue.

Leave the village by lanes leading SW to go directly across the D 945 [IGN 69 slightly inaccurate]. After 200m turn right (SW) off the road by a house onto a path which joins the D 269 which is followed into **Castillon**. Leave that village by a lane running W but S of the D 269, which is rejoined at a bridge and followed to a road junction 1km on. Turn left (S) (sign: *5t*) to join the D 233/263 near **Caubin** (*a Romanesque chapel of the Knights of St John excellently restored*). Turn right to follow the road 1km into the centre of

8km Arthez-de-Béarn 220m

Hotels, restaurants, shops, campsite – 500m south. Buses to Pau, Orthez.

First view of the Pyrenees!

Take the D 275 W for 5km. Turn left just before a double set of pylons onto a stony track before recrossing the road north of **L'Oustalot** to take a track for 1200m, which descends to join the busy N 117. Cross it to pick up the D 275 again across the railway, the *Gave de Pau* and the *autoroute* into

8km Maslacq 80m
Hotel-restaurant, shops
Leave by the D 9 south, after crossing a stream turn left onto a track
SSE ◊ (brown metal arrows), then left again after another 500m ◊,
and a third left ◊ after a gas installation, then right ◊ through maize.
Leave the track at an ivy-covered ruin and turn right, ascending into a
wood, taking the left-hand path of the two to rejoin the track and turn
right. The track joins the D 9 near the access point for **Notre Dame de
Muret**. Cross the road to take the lane leading past **Janet** to a farm,
La Courne, 700m on. Go through the farm buildings then continue
keeping the hedge line and tree belt on the left, after a distance cross
through the trees and ford a stream to reach the farm of *Larqué*
where a lane picks up again – the way is not well marked between the
two farms – and descend with it 2km into

8km Sauvelade 110m
Gîte in preparation in the former abbatial buildings.
   *The church of St Jacques is the remains of an important abbey first
Benedictine, and founded in 1128, and later Cistercian, serving the
pilgrim way through Béarn.*

Take the D 110 S for 1km before turning right at a junction following
the lane uphill through **Chardiesse**, 600m on at a road junction turn
right (NW) passing a beautifully restored building, a fine example of
béarnais vernacular architecture. At the next junction, 500m on,
bear left after a farm house (*Huge Dogs*!) and start to descend.
Turning left, 300m on, to reach a stream, continue W past the farm of
Labarthe to a crossroads 500m later. Turn left (S) to reach a
crossroads near **Boussac** after 1km.
   [The official route links *Labarthe* to **Boussac** across private
property but the paths are not waymarked by agreement and
consequently going astray is easy.] Between **Boussac** and the next
road junction 600m on, the red and white waymarking almost
disappears, giving way to the yellow and red of the *GR de Pays
"Circuit de Gave"*. Continue right, descending through woods S then
W. A lovely fountain of cool sweet water is situated where the road
turns W to reach **Méritein** after 2km, at a junction with the D 947.
Turn off that road left (SSE) to follow the old road parallel into the
eastern outskirts of

12km Navarrenx 130m
*Hotels, restaurants, shops, Syndicat d'Initiative, simple campsite.
Buses to Pau.*
   A bastide on the pilgrimage 'cami' built in 1316; its walls were rebuilt

'in the modern fashion' to accommodate artillery in 1540. *They were again remodelled by Vauban a century later – an attractive town of 1200 lies within them.*

Leave the town by crossing the *Gave D'Oloron*. Turn left onto the D 2 and right off it after 100m to take lanes, crossing the busy D 936, into **Susmiou**. At the west end of the village turn right (N) onto a minor road which 800m later joins the D 115 at a crossroads [IGN 69 is mostly wrong between **Susmiou** and the river *Bidouze* but the way is drearily easy to follow]. Continue W on the D 115, ignoring the yellow and red waymarks which cross the road 700m later, for 6.5km until a junction with the D 160. This is followed N for 1km then a path through a wood is taken NW for 1km, then W onto a lane for 1km to *Bibi*, the unmarked hamlet between **Nabas** and **Rivehaute** (*shop*). There the way turns S to join the D 115 at a crossroads just east of Babas.

[In truth along this dull stretch it is better to continue westwards along the D 115.]

11km Nabas 90m
Café.

Cross the river *Saison* and continue by the D 23 and the D 115 into

6km Aroue 125m
Tabac-confiserie at the Petrol station.

The border between Béarn and the Basque country; the *church of St Etienne* has a sculpted figure of St James mounted, in his guise of the *matamoros*; a representation much more common in Spain.

Leave by the D 11 westwards, turning left (SW) onto a lane at a calvary just past the sign for **Etcharry**. Follow it for about 1500m then turn right (NW) onto a path crossing a field, 500m on a lane is joined and followed N, two left turns reorientate the way W then S to reach

4.5km Olhaïby 120m
Simple Romanesque church.

Continue westwards by the lanes to **Jaureguiberry** then by lanes and tracks SW for 3.5km to a junction with the D 242. Follow this for 1km NW then by a lane W 2km to

8km Larriabar-Sorhapuru 90m
Café-restaurant at D 933 crossroads.

From the village continue NW across the D 933 to a farm, take a track through buildings to a bridge over the river *Bidouze*. The way now becomes much more interesting again having passed through the gentle though uninspiring river valleys of the *Pau* and *Oloron*. Turn

The Stele de Gibraltar with the Pyrenees to the south

left (W) over the bridge to ascend by a path between drystone walls and beneath trees to the village, *Hiriburia*, on the D 302. A monument, the *stèle de Gibraltar*, has been erected here to commemorate the coming together of the three northern French routes, those of *Tours*, *Vézelay* and *Le Puy*, even though its precise location is still subject to historical dispute.

(3km northwards by the D 302 lies **Saint-Palais**, *Hotels, restaurants, shops, campsite, Syndicat d'Initiative. Buses for Bayonne and St-Jean-Pied-de-Port. An attractive and celebrated town on the pilgrim route of which it has a fine little museum.*)

Having crossed the D 302 ascend by a track leading 1500m S to the *Chapelle d'Oyarce* from where there are marvellous Pyrenean vistas. Then descend from near the SE corner of the chapel. A typical Basque memorial cross, a *stèle discoidal*, is passed 800m on, very shortly afterwards go right (W) onto a path off the track arriving 750m later in

5.5km Harambels 160m
A remarkable little Romanesque chapel of St Nicholas is all that remains of an important Benedictine priory-hospital, first mentioned in the XIc. The key for the church is available from Mme Etchevery, one of the hamlet's four surnames that goes back over a thousand

years.

Cross the access road and descend to a stream turning left then right onto a track. At a crossroads go straight across and descend to another stream. A track runs westwards, then a wet stony path is taken into

3.5km Ostabat-Asme 150m
Shops. Gîte at the Maison Ospitalia, the Basque Centre; continuing a tradition when various hospitals and inns could shelter 5000 pilgrims during the Middle Ages.

Leave the village by the minor road leading SW (*Dogs!*). After 1.5km bear right onto a hedged-track. At **Asme-Chilo** ignore two very confusing waymarks that lead one away from the D 933. Join it to continue SW for 800m to **Larcevau-Arros-Cibits** (*Hotels, restaurant, shops.*) Before the cross at the junction going south, turn right onto a tiny road passing a bakery. The way continues by tracks and paths parallel to the D 933 before rejoining it 2.5km later before **Utxiat.** Leave it 250m later to ascend W by a lane to the farm of **Barnetchea**, passing through the farm gates behind the house. Then descend passing wild cherry trees to a stream. The way continues by ascending to a heath then leads SSW, followed by taking a track W into

7.5km Ainhice-Mongelos 200m
Hotel, shop.

At the village crossroads go straight on (W) by lanes for 1500m to join the D 422 which is followed S for 400m. Turn right (W) before the bridge on to a path for 600m, then by lanes S and W 1km to **Bustince**. Continue by minor roads SW to **Irriberry** and then join the D 933 for 850m passing near the bridge the **Chapelle d'Apat Ospitale** (*a XIIc Romanesque remnant of the hospital priory of the Knights of St John.*) Turn right off the busy road, D 933 before the town sign to follow a minor road into the back of

7km Saint-Jean-le-Vieux
Hotels, restaurants, shops, camping.
Originally a Roman foundation, the town and castle were sacked by Richard I. The church was a XIIc building restored in 1630.

The way leaves by a lane off the NW corner of the main square. After 1500m it reaches a junction with the D 933 which it follows for 100m [IGN 69 is inaccurate until **Irunberry**] before turning left off it. A further 100m on turn right (W) to cross the river *Laurhibar* near the church of *Sainte Marie-Madeleine* (*XVc Gothic on the site of a much*

earlier foundation.) The way continues westwards climbing to the *Porte Saint-Jacques*, the traditional pilgrim gate of

4km Saint Jean-Pied-de-Port 180m

Hotels, restaurants, shops, all facilities, campsite, Syndicat d'Initiative. SNCF terminus on the pretty Bayonne line.

An attractive town of 1800 people, straddling the river Nive; the upper town has only really one street, the cobbled rue de la Citadelle, which contains the fascinating bishop's prison, now a museum. The lower town, the walls, Porte d'Espagne and the massive citadel were built in 1688 by Vauban. The town only became French in 1659, having been ceded by Spain at the Treaty of the Pyrenees along with Roussillon. The XIVc Gothic church sits on the river bank.

Leave by the *Porte d'Espagne* to follow the road known as the *route Napoleon*, though its antiquity is far greater, having been a prehistoric tin route and later a link on the Roman road joining *Bordeaux* to *Astoria*. After 4km the hamlet of **Hountto** (alt. 500m) is passed, and a short cut zig-zags off the left to join the road again some distance higher up. It is now possible to walk on the wide grassy verges with increasingly wider views over *Navarre*. After another 3.5km a stream is crossed and the trans-Pyrenean walk the GR 10 joins from the right. The paths are coincident for 1km until a junction dominated by a statue of the virgin of *Orisson* at 1140m. From here far off to the left the peaks above the valley of the *Aspe* and the *Somport* pass – the pass for the fourth and most southerly of the major French routes, that from *Italy-Arles-Toulouse* – tower up well over 2000m.

Take the right fork, continuing on the road verges for 3.5km, passing the ruins of the XVc Spanish fort of *Château-Pignon* on the left, until at a well-marked point the route bears right, away from the road onto a grassy path. 1km on the border is reached; on the Spanish side lies a beechwood, fenced off. Follow the fence SE for 400m then near the border marker number 199 cross into

SPAIN

15km Col de Bentartea 1337m

The waymarking for the *Camino de Santiago*, for that is what the *Chemin de St Jacques* has now become, from here for the 680km to *Compostela* is by means of yellow flashes and marks.

After 3.5km a track is joined at the *Port de Cize*, the highpoint of the route at 1480m. There are tremendous views south into *Navarra*.

The Way of St James descending through beeches
below the Port de Cize

The Pyrenean passes linking France and Spain seen from below Roncesvalles

Follow the waymarked route left through woods on the course of a Roman road to

7km Roncesvalles 960m

Hotel-restaurant Casa Sabina and the monastery-run posada, which is expensive for Spain. Walker pilgrims may stay in the monastery's guest dormitory, they may also receive an 'itinerario' from the vice-Abbott. This 'passport' contains pages for stamps or 'sellos' which are obtained at the historic waypoints of the camino. When completed and presented at the cathedral in Santiago it secures one an authentic 'compostela', the certificate of the pilgrimage.

The 'valley of thorns' contains the Augustinian monastery, once known as the gateway to Spain; it was refounded about 1230 by Sancho the Strong of Navarra, the principal victor over the Andalusian muslims at Las Navas de Tolosa in 1212. As well as containing his enormous tomb (he himself was 7 foot tall) and that of his wife Clemencia, the monastery also displays the battle flags, captured from the muslims. The church today is French Gothic atop Spanish Romanesque. Its cloisters date from after 1400, the earlier ones having been destroyed in a fire. Within the complex there is a treasury that boasts as many relics as **Conques**, *a simple XIIIc chapel* *of St James and a more elaborate one, altered in the XVc, dedicated to Espíritu Santo.*

One mile north is the pass of Ibaneta, forever associated with Roland and the destruction of Charlemagne's rearguard, allegedly by 'moors'. In fact it was the native Basques harrying the King's forces following the unwarranted sack of their capital **Pamplona** in 778. Nonetheless, a monument here too commemorates another psychologically necessary myth, so that there is one at both ends of the Camino de Santiago. The 'Chanson de Roland' became one of medieval Europe's most famous and popular 'gestes'.

40km onwards and downhill lies **Pamplona**, a good day's walk and quite different from anything north of the Pyrenees. For continuing into Spain and **Santiago** see Appendix II.

Ultreia!

APPENDICES

APPENDIX I

The southern route of about 19km across the *Aubrac* links **Rieutort d'Aubrac** with **Aubrac**. It is only waymarked, officially, as far as **Marchastel**, and between the large lake immediately east of the D 219, SE of spot height *1375m* and **Aubrac**. Between the D 52 and D 219 a former Roman road is followed passing the site of *Ad Silanum*. The route is marked on IGN 58.

Rieutort d'Aubrac

Do not turn right to follow the new road, but go straight through the village leaving the communal ovens and the fountains on the right. The fine old road leads in 1km to **Marchastel**. Cross the D 900 and continue for 2km on the hard white track over a stone bridge to the farm of *Puech-Palat* (sign). There are two discreet waymarks just before the farm. Turn left then right through (that French favourite) a barbed wire gate. Then either follow the electricity/telephone lines through the trough of the ground (boggy), or go left (E) to follow a drystone wall that leads S along the ridge. Both lead to a cliff of granite crowned by a cross overlooking the **Lac de St Andiol** at *1225m*. Follow the tarmac road westwards to the junction with the D 52 (sign: *Buron et Lac de BORN*). Turn right to follow it N, crossing the bridge over the *Ruisseau de Plèches*. Continue a little way before crossing a tumbledown drystone wall and barbed wire fence. Climb the hill, spot height *1276m*, immediately in front to the west, in order to reach two barns or *burons*.

  Continue W then NW to a gap in the thin line of a fir plantation, where there is a barbed wire gate; there is also a fading waymark here. Follow a grassy track uphill, the ancient Roman road; the track bears left (S) as it climbs. It is easy to follow to the site of *Ad Silanum*, where the collapsing trenches of former archaeological excavations may be seen; following it thereafter is more difficult. The route continues to climb and veers increasingly S, two streams are forded and then a stile (very unusual in France!) leads across a barbed wire fence. The Roman road is now again much clearer. Cross a stream and go through two more barbed wire gates to reach a farm road, turn right (W) along it to join the D 219. Take it S for 500m before turning right (NW) over a barbed wire gate ◊ *Tour de l'Aubrac.*

The contrast either side of the D 219 is amazing: east is essentially a treeless pennine-like plateau, west is hanging woodland. The path is now well waymarked below the scarp-line of cliffs and beech hengars to descend to a stream, where the going is rather boggy. After a second stream the way ascends steeply by a drove road to enter **Aubrac** from the south on the D 533.

APPENDIX II
Onwards into Spain

The way on is as good a journey, more so even, than that which has gone before. There will be more people underway and a greater awareness of what the walker is about. The waymarking is by means of yellow flashes and marks, even by ribbons in *Navarra*. In *Galicia* itself UNESCO is erecting ½km stones of granite, eventually these will stretch back to the French border.

Maps are a problem in Spain, even those issued for army usage; they are very, very difficult to obtain and even at 1:100 000 can be inaccurate. The Spanish publishers, Everest, produce a book that is cheap, 800psts (£4) and universally available, *El Camino de Santiago: Guía del Peregrino*. This, in absence of anything else, is the guide to the way. While it is in Spanish there is much that can be gleaned by the non-linguist, but more importantly, it contains maps of the route. These are schematic rather than accurate projections but they have only a few inaccuracies and are very easy to follow, even through the larger towns. With this the only extra maps needed would be, say, Michelin 42 and 441 to give a larger overview. A recently published French volume *Le Chemin de Saint Jacques de Compostelle: Guide Pratique de Pelerin en Espagne* by Abbe Georges Bernès, Georges Veron and Louis Laborde Balen, published by Editions Randonnées Pyrénéennes (1986) contains much interesting information but cannot be recommended as a guide to the route as it is at present waymarked. It can however, unlike the Everest *Guía*, be bought in Britain.

Other important information, indeed up-to-the-moment information, can be found in the Confraternity of St James' indispensable and annually updated handbook *The Pilgrim Guide to Spain*, (£2.50 in 1988). *Los Amigos del Camino de Santiago* based in *Estella* publish lists of *refugios* for walkers and will issue *itinerarios* tor any starting point on the way in Spain. Addresses of both organisations are given in the following appendix.

APPENDIX III

Bibliography

D. J. Hall	English Medieval Pilgrimage, 1966
M. F. Hearn	Romanesque Sculpture, 1981
Rob Hunter	Walking in France, 1983
T. A. Layton	The Way of St James: Pilgrim Roads to Santiago de Compostela, 1976
Edwin Mullins	Pilgrimage to Santiago, 1975
A. K. Porter	Romanesque Sculpture of the Pilgrimage Roads, 1923
Walter Starkie	Road to Santiago, 1953
Jonathan Sumption	Pilgrimage: An Image of Medieval Religion, 1975

Useful Addresses

Confraternity of St James
57 Leopold Road
London N2 8BG

(Hon. Sec. Pat Quaife   Tel: 01-883 4893)

Los Amigos del Camino de Santiago
Apartado de Correos, 20
Estella
Navarra

GLOSSARY

Auvergnat and Gascon are dialects of French; Occitan is a separate Romance language rooted in Spanish, Catalan and Italian.

Auvergnat

aven, igue	swallow-hole
brandes	heather, broom, bracken moor
castel	manor house
cingle	river meander, loop
cloup, gouffre	solution hole
gariotte	drystone circular cell
lauze	thick stone roofing slate
lande	heath
serre	long narrow ridge
sotch	large solution hole

Gascon

barthe	humid wood
bernet	alder wood
caoune	dale
cassague	oak forest
castagnère	chestnut wood
haget	beech wood
lane	heather
paguère	north side of a hill
peyrère	quarry
pouy, pitè, tuc	hill
soulan, arrajadé	hill sides open to the sun

Occitan

barry	suburb
cami, caminol	way, road
calade	paved (often of a Roman road)
clédo	paling fence
conques	dale
coudere	meadow, enclosure
fromental	wheatfield (lt. *fromentaria*)
pau	fortified enclosure
pech	hill
soleilho	open-sided loft for grain storage

Basque

aitz, haytz	oak
aran, ibar	valley
arri, harri	stone
beltz	black

bide	path
borda	farm
celhay, zelhay	plateau
chara	wood
chipi, chiqui	small
churi	white
cuby	bridge
elhorri	pine
erreka	stream
etche	house
goyen, gora	high
handi	large
hegi	hill, bank
ithurri	fountain
larra, larria	heath
lepo	col, pass

Place name study is often fraught with difficulty but in general those villages/settlements suffixed *-ac* or *-an*, eg. Figeac, are of Gallo-Roman foundation. Those suffixed *-ens*, eg. Flamarens, are Germanic, Frankish or Visigothic; some earlier villages may be refoundations or renamed so it is not always a reliable guide for the earliest date of historical establishment.

CICERONE PRESS GUIDES

Cicerone publish a range of reliable guides to walking and climbing in Europe

FRANCE
TOUR OF MONT BLANC
CHAMONIX MONT BLANC - A Walking Guide
TOUR OF THE OISANS: GR54
WALKING THE FRENCH ALPS: GR5
THE CORSICAN HIGH LEVEL ROUTE: GR20
ROCK CLIMBS IN THE VERDON
THE WAY OF ST. JAMES: GR65

FRANCE/SPAIN
WALKS & CLIMBS IN THE PYRENEES

SPAIN
WALKING IN MALLORCA
WALKS & CLIMBS IN THE PICOS DE EUROPA

FRANCE/SWITZERLAND
THE JURA - Walking the High Route and Winter Ski Traverses

SWITZERLAND
WALKS IN THE ENGADINE
THE VALAIS - A Walking Guide

GERMANY/AUSTRIA
THE KALKALPEN TRAVERSE
KLETTERSTEIG - Scrambles in the Northern Limestone Alps
MOUNTAIN WALKING IN AUSTRIA
WALKING IN THE SALZKAMMERGUT
KING LUDWIG WAY

ITALY
ALTA VIA - High Level Walks in the Dolomites
VIA FERRATA - Scrambles in the Dolomites
ITALIAN ROCK - Selected Rock Climbs in Northern Italy
CLASSIC CLIMBS IN THE DOLOMITES

OTHER AREAS
THE MOUNTAINS OF GREECE - A Walker's Guide
TREKS & CLIMBS in the mountains of Rhum and Petra, JORDAN
CRETE: OFF THE BEATEN TRACK
ATLAS MOUNTAINS

GENERAL OUTDOOR BOOKS
LANDSCAPE PHOTOGRAPHY
FIRST AID FOR HILLWALKERS
MOUNTAIN WEATHER
JOURNEY AFTER DAWN
MOUNTAINEERING LITERATURE
SKI THE NORDIC WAY- A Manual of Cross-Country Skiing
THE ADVENTURE ALTERNATIVE

CANOEING
SNOWDONIA WILD WATER, SEA & SURF
WILDWATER CANOEING

CARTOON BOOKS
ON FOOT & FINGER
ON MORE FEET & FINGERS
LAUGHS ALONG THE PENNINE WAY

CICERONE PRESS

Also a full range of guide-books to walking, scrambling, ice-climbing, rock climbing, and other adventurous pursuits in Britain and abroad.

Other guides are constantly being added to the Cicerone List. Available from bookshops, outdoor equipment shops of direct (send for price list) from CICERONE PRESS, 2 POLICE SQUARE, MILNTHORPE CUMBRIA LA7 7PY

Printed by Carnmor Print & Design,
95/97, London Road, Preston, Lancashire.